Winning

Hysteria 2016 Writing Competition

The Hysterectomy Association.

Edited by Linda Parkinson-Hardman

Hysteria 5

Published by: The Hysterectomy Association

ISBN: 978-0-9927429-9-7

A catalogue record for this book is available from The British Library.

Telephone: 0843 289 2142

Website: www.hysterectomy-association.org.uk

About the Hysteria Writing Competition

Hysteria is an annual writing competition for women only; it opens on the 1st April each year and closes at midnight on the 31st August. You can find out more about the competition, including rules and guidelines for entries on the Hysterectomy Association website about the next competition at: www.HysteriaUK.co.uk.

Acknowledgements

The competition and this anthology wouldn't have been possible without the support and help of our amazing volunteer judges.

This book is dedicated to them and to the users of the Hysterectomy Association.

Judges

Short Stories:

Pat Good	Carol Warham
Catherine Menon	Anne Wilson
Hannah Onoguwe	Marcia Woolf

Flash Fiction:

Alex Reece Abbott	Stephanie Hutton
Veronica Bright	Ingrid Jedrezekjewski
Helen Chambers	Sherry Morris

Poetry:

Tessa Foley	Mary Oliver
Beatriz Menedez	Julie Turley
Lynda Nash	

Foreword

This is the fifth year of the Hysteria Writing Competition. When we began, it was with a single competition in mind, since then it's grown beyond our original expectations and is now a major part of the Hysterectomy Association year.

Its purpose is threefold; to help raise funds for the work we do through the association; to produce another book we can add to our collection for purchase by our users and visitors; and perhaps most importantly, it introduces to women who might otherwise never know we exist and who might need our help, information and support in the future.

Every year we work with the same loose theme, things of interest to women. Every year I am stunned and humbled by the breadth and vitality the entries breath into common issues. Our judges receive so many fantastic entries that it's almost impossible for them to slide a sliver of paper between them; often only fractions of a point separate the top ten in each category from their fellows.

In this anthology, we continue the tradition we began two years ago and include a selection of advice from our judges. They have a wealth of writing, competition and publishing experience that you can draw on in the future.

Linda

6

Contents

Flash fiction

The Flash Fiction category was open to entries with a maximum word count of 250 words. These ultra-short stories needed to be complete and give the reader the satisfaction of not being left hanging.

The challenge when writing flash fiction is to tell a complete story in which every word is essential. It's important that the writer pares down the padding, peels away the layers and ends up with the pure essence of the story.

Advice from our Flash Fiction Judges

Helen Chambers

http://wivenhoewriters.blogspot.co.uk/p/helen-chambers.html

Flash fiction is such a brilliant form both to read, and to write in. Every word must count, so there should never be any waffle or fluff: powerful verbs and precise nouns carry a clear story. The trick is to evoke a strong sense of place, an atmosphere or feeling into the shortest of stories – and there does need to be a story, a narrative arc. The reader needs to be transported and not notice the writing! I loved reading this year's entries, and many of them stayed with me long afterwards (the true sign of successful flash fiction). It was a pleasure and a privilege to be a judge.

Veronica Bright

www.veronicabright.co.uk

Work hard on your piece of writing to make it stand out from the crowd. Yes, that's easier said than done, because there's a lot of talent out there, but be positive. Each one of us is given many opportunities to learn. Find answers to the following questions, and face the opposition more confidently.

- Could you approach your theme from a new and intriguing angle? Your goal is to make a competition judge think, 'Ah, this sounds very interesting.'
- Is your opening line as riveting as it could be? Entice your reader in.
- Does your middle continue to hold the reader's attention?
- Have you written a satisfying end?
- Have you used creative language to enhance your work? Make your judge think, 'I wish I'd thought of that.'
- Have you edited your work several times? A good idea is to write a first draft, put it aside for a few days, and then work through it slowly and carefully.
- Have you read your work aloud to make sure it flows well?
- Have you asked a trusted, honest friend for their opinion? They may be able to spot a pitfall that you've missed.
- Have you checked all the rules? If you haven't followed them carefully, you might as well go outside and post your entrance fee down the nearest drain.

Winning a prize or making a shortlist is exciting and satisfying, a tremendous boost to confidence. So, keep on entering competitions. Refuse to give up.

Alex Reece Abbott

www.alexreeceabbott.info

First of all, thank you and congratulations for sending your work – that's always a milestone.

Of course, any judging is highly subjective. To even things out, we were asked to consider aspects including:- imagery; grammar, punctuation and spelling; originality; drama; a clear theme or message; the language and clichés; the old "show rather than tell" maxim; the distinctiveness of voice; the structure – a clear beginning, middle and end; and how satisfied we were on reading the piece.

And, not least, how much we enjoyed the work.

Flash fiction is a demanding form. Generally, the stories that most grabbed me started with a strong, fresh title, one that added something to the piece as a whole. Somehow that signals to your readers that you know what you want to say. Opening lines - and opening words - are so important. And so too, the ending and that last paragraph and/or line; don't leave your reader hanging. Edit them for impact.

A few stories really stood out with their original idea or an original approach. If you are writing about a common experience, like relationship problems, then find a fresh angle to disrupt our expectations and bring some drama. If it's highly personal to you, consider making the voice third person, to give yourself more distance as a writer. Be fresh and specific with your word choices, and use them to create the mood you want to evoke and to engage your readers. I'd like to see more humourous stories too – and stories that include humour to help convey their message. As writers, we are always learning – could any of these aspects of your story be sharpened up? Small changes can make a big difference.

If you didn't make the cut this time, then I URGE you to take a fresh look at your story. Tweak it and keep going, submit it some more. And, keep reading the work of other flash writers. It's amazing what you can learn in one page. Good luck!

Ingrid Jendrzejewski

www.ingridj.com

It was an honour and privilege to read all the work submitted – and so exciting to see all the different approaches authors had to writing flash fiction.

Overall, the stories that grabbed me most were the ones that experimented with unique subjects, fresh language and innovative narrative techniques. The stories that relied too heavily on a 'trick' or 'twist' ending didn't tend to stand up to multiple readings unless something else was going on, and stories on common themes (like failing romantic relationships) had to do extra work to stand out.

As for the stories that were nearly there, several could have been improved with better editing. In flash fiction, every word of every sentence needs to carry its weight. If it's not integral to the story, it should be changed or ruthlessly cut! The title, first line and last line carry extra punch, so it's worth spending the time perfecting these.

It was extraordinarily difficult to sift through all the pieces that were submitted, and my congratulations go to all the brilliant writers included in this anthology.

Sea Change

Sharon Telfer

My heart sank.

I watched it go. It fought hard to keep afloat. I took my boathook, knocked back its jellyfish pulses. I had to make sure. Cracked, it bubbled silver as it dropped, an aspirin fizz then one toxic gulp like mercury breaking from a thermometer. It stopped struggling after that, twisted, turned in the tug of the tide, spiralling slowly down into the deep dark.

I watched until I could see it no more.

My mother warned me. You never know when you might want it back. To shut her up, I marked it by the harbour buoy. I knew I wouldn't need it again. I crossed off years well enough without it, the sea coming in, going out, working, eating, sleeping. Except on stormy nights. The wild clamour of the buoy bell woke me then. I'd hug the pillow over my ears and curse my mother.

But she was right. Of course.

There you were, one day, end of the pier, leaning into the wind like a figurehead. For the first time since I drowned my heart, I licked my roughened, seaside lips and tasted salt.

That night I rowed out and let down my net. I threw back the crabs and the mackerel, rubbed off the barnacle crust by the light of the moon. My pearlescent heart shone, strange, hard, beautiful.

I bent my back to the oars and headed for land, heart thumping like a fresh caught fish.

Sharon Telfer won the June 2016 Bath Flash Fiction Award and has a story in this year's National Flash Fiction Day anthology. She cut her flash fiction teeth winning the @AdHocFiction and @FaberAcademy weekly competitions. She works as a non-fiction writer and editor, translating social policy research into everyday English.

Twitter: @sharontelfer

Sleeping Dogs

Irene Buckler

He bursts headlong into our lives, a slippery squalling infant, and she, who has longed for a child for so long, emerges from childbirth triumphant. A mother, at last, she draws me close and wraps me in the moment with her. This is where our new life as a family can begin.

Beguiled by this tiny human with his downy halo of baby hair and miniature hands that instinctively curl around my forefinger as if he is staking a claim, I sense the possibilities, but I am uncertain. Will he be a cure for what ails us or a just sticking plaster on the festering wound of our disappointments? Childlessness, the source of all the tension between us for so long, will no longer be the issue. The issue now is how we deal with our secrets. I know her secret, but she doesn't know mine. However, she recognises my hesitation.

"I love you so much, Tom," she reassures me, her eyes bright with emotion, "and you will be the best father in world. I know it. "

This is neither the time to tell her that I am sterile nor to discuss infidelity, but she is right. I will be a good father.

We name our son Thomas.

As a teacher for over three decades, **Irene Buckler** wrote many educational programs, stories for children and poetry, some of which have appeared in publications for children in the United Kingdom and Australia. Irene enjoys the challenge of writing flash fiction where less is so much more.

Twiller: @glenwoodize

Waiting for the Big One

Marie Gethins

When my chair shook, I thought of you and curled up, knees to chest. My book slapped the wooden floor. I stopped breathing, but your baritone snores drifted across the room—even, steady. I thanked a higher power. The whiskey bottle and glass chimed, jitterbugging together along the coffee table. The light shade pendulumed over your head. Years ago in Walmart, I thought it looked like an exploding star—a silver ball with a multitude of rays. Now as it circled, I saw a mace and wondered if the electric cable might just snap.

Seconds ticking, vibrations continued to roll, intensity increasing. I jumped out of the chair and touched your shoulder. 'Earthquake,' I said. 'EARTHQUAKE.'

Your eyelids flickered for a moment. I stepped back from your glare. You looked up and focused on the swirling ball. 'So what.' Twisting into the couch, you dismissed me.

It's been two hours since you sprayed my face with spittle, the words pelting me until your palm sent my head pointing in another direction. You laughed when I touched my swelling cheek, gave promises of more next time. Next time.

The room continued to rumble. I moved under a door frame. Braced in my narrow haven, I imagined a fissure swallowing the couch, bottle and you. A silver comet followed your descent, exploding and filling the room with a rainbow of light. I whispered a prayer and hoped it was the Big One.

Marie Gethins won/placed in The Short Story, Tethered by Letters, Flash500, Dromineer, The New Writer, Prick of the Spindle and 99fiction.net. Other pieces listed in Boulevard, Bath, Bristol, Brighton, Fish Short Story/Flash/Memoir, James Plunkett, and RTE/Penguin com¬pe¬ti¬tions. Marie is a Pushcart, Best of the Short Fictions, and British Screenwriters Award Nominee.

@MarieGethins

Octopus

Gwen Sayers.

Lucy wades in the green, foot dip. Chlorine steams. Her mother paces beside the pool, stilettos clipping the tiles.

'Two lengths today.'

The small girl tugs her costume over her tummy. 'I feel sick.'

Her mother's lips are wounded strips. 'Don't lie.'

Lucy clings, pudgy-fingered, to the handrails. She drops, rung by rung, to her knees, waist, shoulders. She clutches the gutter's rim, shivering. The deep end ripples in the distance, hiding the octopus. She pushes away. Teeth chatter, arms splatter, she swims a few yards before grasping the side, peering. Nothing. She churns on, stopping to rest – to scout.

The octopus still lurks, bobbing and humming, against the wall beneath the trough. She swims near as she dares and grabs the gutter. Her mother said there couldn't be an octopus in the pool, stupid, they live in the ocean.

The octopus floats towards her, long and shadowy. She must be meddling. She lets go, hoping to swim clear before she has to stop again. She thrashes the water, holding her breath, clamping her eyelids. She found the rubbery snake in a drawer by her mother's bed. It buzzed when she touched it. Her mother slammed the drawer; said the creature was an octopus that swallowed little girls who meddled.

She can't tell if she's swum far enough. The water feels thick as dough. Her legs sink, arms flail. She opens her eyes. Her mother was wrong. The octopus is spreading, filling the pool with darkness.

Gwen Sayers was born in Johannesburg and lives in London. Her writing has been published in Hysteria, Fish Anthology, Mslexia, and Structo. She was shortlisted for the Bridport Prize 2015 and came second in the Fish Short Memoir Prize 2016.

www.gwensayers.com

Boudicca

Karen Money

Boudicca lives in my head.

She's restless and beautiful. Her hair swishes and her sword glints.

I'm peeling potatoes at the kitchen table. I need to be ready to fry when he comes home. My hands are rough and red against the scrubbed pine table. Worn hands. Obedient hands. Hands that tremble sometimes.

The potatoes are chipped and parboiled. I scrape the peelings into the bin and scrub my hands with lemon soap. I sniff them. The lemon never quite masks the raw potato smell, however often I wash them. Our son hates chips.

He left home last week.

I sit at the table and wait. My fingers tap out a staccato rhythm on the table. I slow them down. I can't slow my heartbeat though.

The front door slams. He lurches into the room. Something's wrong.

'I miss our lad,' he says, 'Let's make another. Tea can wait.'

He yanks a handful of my hair to his face and inhales noisily.

The bars are bending. The gap is widening.

He licks my cheek like a dog.

And Boudicca smashes her fist into his face.

The pain in my hand is excruciating. But the shock in his eyes is glorious. His fists clench. Boudicca grabs her sword and shrieks an unearthly battle cry.

He goes pale and drops into a chair.

Boudicca laughs and her sword clangs to the floor. I open the front door. The air is cool and enticing. I step out into the evening.

Karen Money has two adult children and works as a vocal coach in Devon. She has been songwriting for years and only stumbled into writing fiction more recently. She is currently working on her first novel while trying hard to ignore ideas for the next one.

www.tavistocksingingteacher.co.uk

Batman and Unicorns

Natalie Poyser

I hide Unicorns.

Pictures of them, that is. In a 300-page report, it's amazing what you can sneak in. Who reads past the Executive Summary anyway?

The new guy, Jacob – Altman? Alderman? – from upstairs, swings past my desk. "Have you got the proofs for the community engagement event flyers?"

I nod. I'm a marketing team of one and I'm very efficient at my job. "Sure."

"And is that the latest report?"

I pass him a copy, hiding a smile. Nobody ever notices my tiny additions.

He admires my Unicorn mug, and grins. "Nice!"

After lunch, Gary stalks past my desk. "Can you do the meeting minutes upstairs? Alice is sick."

I sigh, but follow him. Boot up my laptop. Jacob slots into the seat beside me. He's still grinning. Widely. I'm supposed to be paying attention, but as the others talk, Jacob slowly flicks through the report, to pages he has marked. I bob my gaze over.

He's circled every single Unicorn.

I accidentally hit DELETE and ruin my minutes.

It's only when I'm back at my desk I see his hand-written note on the report's last page.

Good work, Unicorn girl. But can you find Batman...?!

It takes me all evening. On the penultimate page, on the small but obligatory team photo, Batman is photo-shopped into the back row. Even I didn't spot it, and I cropped and added all the photos. I check the tiny photo credits line.

Natalie Poyser is an administrator, musician and writer who lives in Edinburgh. Her poetry and short fiction have been published in New Writing Scotland, Poetry Scotland, the Scottish Herald, and Writing Magazine. Her YA novel Make Believe was shortlisted for the 2016 Wells Festival of Literature Story for Children prize.

Helix Aspersa

Vicki Morley

I am ...a trifle crushed, my petticoat, corset, muslin sprigged dress, blue satin slippers are squeezing inwards. My breasts round as oriental oranges are shrinking, my auburn curls are floating away. I drop my clove-studded pomander as I see my feet are widening, moving together. Spring sunshine is burning my shrivelling arms.

I seek refuge in the dappled shade of the kitchen garden. I look down, my eyes sting. I am spiralling, dwindling and shrinking. I must be suffering from an ague. An ague definitely, there was that frolic with the ambassador from the Low Countries. I need to lie down.

I wake to discover an outrage, a horror beyond comprehension. My feet welded together are the size and colour of a house mouse. No fur, but a hideous crusting shell house. My eyes that were the delight of the court, are revolting elastic horns that zoom above and below the leaves.

I can no longer sing or speak, my tongue is a toothed radula set in my hideous foot. I peer behind and spot a river of slime emanating from my foot. This is outrageous, I am uglier than the Duchess of Carlisle.

Thank goodness I am hidden by this large hosta leaf. Wait a minute; I can crawl up the stem, look I am swivelling sideways, now upside down. I feel a little giddy but the leaf looks as refreshing as a generous glass of claret. Let's try, yes, succulent verdant juice. Another bite or two or three.

Vicki Morley lives in Penzance and enjoys the Penzance Literary Festival held annually in July, plus the town boasts an independent bookshop called, The Edge of the World. This is apt as we are at the end of the line and many poets and writers have washed up here!

What Doesn't Kill You

Laura Bridge

That old pipe had drip-dripped away, rotting the bathroom floorboards until they couldn't take any more. We found Mum in the kitchen below. Still in the bath.

"It's lucky nobody was making dinner," the coroner said, "or she'd have taken them with her."

The bath was ruined. I dragged it up the garden, vaguely considering filling it with flowers, in memory.

When my husband was finally found out, he stormed off in such a rage he drove into the garden fence.

I didn't argue when the girls said they didn't want to see him again.

"You'll regret this," he said. I wasn't sure.

The fence posts ended up dumped in the bath at the top of the garden. I got a new fence.

"Don't take it personally. It's redundancy, not sacking," my drycleaner store boss said. That sounds worse. Redundant: useless.

They gave me a tablecloth to say goodbye. Like I hadn't seen enough linen in the job. I chucked it in the bath up the garden with the other unhappy memories.

The flood caught everyone unprepared. Cars, cows, people washing down the street. Like the tornado scene in Wizard of Oz, only wetter and less funny.

I bundled the kids outside and into the bathtub. Wrapped in the tablecloth, I used the fence posts as oars. We drifted, watching the devastation and singing the lullabies Mum had sung to comfort us all as babes.

"What doesn't kill you makes you stronger," she'd told me.

I'm beginning to believe it.

Laura Bridge loves the challenge and precision of writing flash fiction. She has a Masters of Education in Children's Literature and has taught in primary schools in Spain, The Netherlands and England. Laura currently lives in Bath with her husband and two sons and is enjoying writing longer stories for children.

Twitter: @laurabridge

Skinny Dipping

Josephine L. Martin

Loch Morar, August 1953. Slick skin over ripe flesh, pressing together beneath the surface until we almost split. We let the sun dry us, then leap in again.

The river by your Dad's allotment, June 1957. You gash your leg on a broken bicycle. Blood billows and disappears. I patch you up. We lie. We heave out the bicycle and dump it in the hawthorns.

Windermere, October 1964. You have to push me in. Chests heave and limbs flail, failing to break the cold. We fold into a blanket that smells of wax and woodsmoke and watch the sky bloom red. Months later, a rose blossoms.

Grafham Water, July 1980, the time we are caught. He shouts, we're not teenagers any more. We sprint back to the car hand in hand like teenagers, thinking of the one left behind. My tears spill anger, mostly.

The stream at the bottom of our village, April 1999. We're just paddling, sharp shingle biting. Holding each other against the haunting sweep of the tide, watching shadows in patchwork windows. The night is never as dark when you are outside, inside it.

The chair by the bath, December 2015. The scar runs down your shin as if drawn with bone not flesh. You giggle as I kiss it, pretending it's the first time. I help you thread your feet into your pyjamas. You rise in three motions then offer me your arm, and we wade across the landing, bare feet tickling the soft carpet bed.

Josephine L. Martin is a scientist on maternity leave, enjoying the opportunity to do some writing while breastfeeding her daughter. She started writing in June 2016. She has flash fiction forthcoming in Halo, and her work was highly commended in the recent Ouse Washes Poetry Competition.

Twitter: @JosephineWriter

The Sound of One Page Ripping

Jude Higgins

A rush of winter air as the door opens and Amanda comes into the cafe, a thin, freckled woman with nervous eyes. She looks like her profile picture. Tick. Smiles when she recognises me. Tick. Two minutes late. Cross. Orders a croissant and eats it without spilling crumbs. Tick. 'Most people call me Mandy.' Cross. Mandies, Debbies – all the same – fluff, not grit. But her voice sounds more growl than budgie. Tick. Hacks Linux. Tick, tick. She loves reading. Tick. Enjoys films. Tick. Has she seen 'The Lobster?' Verdict? 'Everyone's favourite dating satire,' she says. 'But not mine.' Cross. Didn't she think it was hilarious? 'If you like sadism and animal cruelty.' Her gaze is steady, no nervous flicker now. Tick. It's time for me to bring out the novel. This week, 'A Diary of A Nobody'. 'Another satirical view on society,' I say. 'Of the gentler kind.' Amanda relaxes. Yes, she read it years ago. It's funny. Tick. Would she like to read some of it now? She looks surprised but leans in close enough for me to inhale her perfume (musky, with hints of burnt vanilla). Tick. I open the book at random, like I always do, slowly rip out a page and hand it across. Amanda recoils. Cross.Cross.Cross. 'Have to dash,' she says rummaging in her bag. I don't bother to answer. I'm already checking my emails.

Jude Higgins has won or been placed in several flash fiction competitions and among other places, is published in Flash Frontier, The Blue Fifth Review, The New Flash Fiction Review, Halo and Severine magazines, National Flash Fiction Day Anthologies and Visual Verse. She runs Bath Flash Fiction Award.

www.judehiggins.com

Poetry

The poetry category sought entries which had a maximum of 20 lines, not including spaces. Many of our entries followed a strict rule of either four or five line stanzas, but a few challenged this convention.

Poetry is not something that can easily be defined; but it is a written form which lends itself to being spoken out loud. Sometimes, it is easier to understand poetry when you hear it, rather than read it because the rhythm and emphasis of the words can be more easily defined.

The poet's challenge is to create a strong visual image and emotional reaction in the reader or listener.

Advice from our poetry judges

Tessa Foley

www.tessafoley.com

Be reckless. Let your mind go blank and write with abandon, letting your initial ideas splurge out. Only show control when you return to your draft to edit, at which point, do not be afraid to turf something out if it doesn't fit (if you love a line that much, save it for a piece in to which it fits!). Make sure you read through your finished poem several times, aloud ideally, hearing how it scans; also try asking a friend to read it back to you. And ultimately, believe in your work and submit! You can't be recognised if you don't show your work so share it, send it, enter it and trust it.

Julie Turley

Raising funds to support Warwick in Africa - www.justgiving.com/Julie-Hurlston

It has been a great honour and a pleasure to be a judge in the poetry section of the Hysteria Poetry Competition 2016. It is wonderful to see the great wealth of talent that we have and to know that the wonderful tradition of telling stories through poetry lives on.

Poetry can be a real outpouring of the emotions, a valve for the frustrations and stresses of life. When writing I would always advise you to keep it real. Write what you know about and don't worry to much about the technicalities. Obviously spelling and punctuation are important but it is also important that you give your words and thoughts the chance to flow.

The subject of the poems has ranged from hanging out washing to the pain of loss, how wonderful. Don't ever think that any subject matter is too mundane, you are chronicling your story and that of the age we live in. Write as yourself, don't try to be clever with big words that would never usually pass your lips.

To the winners, well done, I hope that this has inspired you to continue to write. To all, keep writing, keep telling your story, for yourselves and for us.

Mary Oliver

If a theme is provided, I might write freely around it first; I'd write masses. Using the automatic writing technique's not a bad idea (writing for 10 minutes without thinking and without stopping, at all); continuous prose; allowing my imagination to take over; censor nothing. Put it aside. Repeat the process the next day. And the next. On the third day, I read through all the garbage I've written and high-light the really surprising, interesting words and phrases. I write the first draft of a poem using those words and phrases (adding others if I want to). I take a pair of scissors and cut, or carefully rip, the poem up into its component lines. I chuck them in the air. Then see if the haphazard arrangement of lines on the floor throws a new light on the matter. Now I might feel ready to start writing the poem.

No theme? I might still start by writing freely and automatically - a 'theme' will emerge, depending on where I am (geographically, emotionally, etc). The content will reveal itself at some point. Then I follow a similar process as described above. I like tricking myself in this way. But it's only a way of getting started. The crafting and editing and work-shopping that follows usually lasts about ten years. By which time I've missed the deadline. But hey, I wrote a fab poem once!

Soapbox

Kathryn V. Jacopi

If I could, I'd travel backwards in time to an 1816 bustling seaport. I'd
wear jelly shoes
and a long t-shirt donning me in a cartoon bikini
—that'd totally freak 'em out.
I'd find a crate,
step up and
shout:
VAGINA
VAGINA
They'd
arrest me and
I'd be the headline:
Immodest Lunatic Woman Shouts
Profanity. Before flash-backing home, I'd stop by
the press just for the artist's rendition of the bikini-clad babe with
freaky-deaky jellies.

Kathryn V. Jacopi, an English professor at Fairfield University, has an MFA in writing from Fairfield University and an MS in special education from Southern Connecticut State University. Her writing has appeared in The Elm City Review and online at Cease, Cows. She was accepted into the One Story Emergent Writers Workshop, 2013.

www.facebook.com/KathrynV.Jacopi

Dizzy With It

Mandy Huggins

We wrote our songs on Saturdays
after Chelsea Girl and the Wimpy Bar,
lyrics strewn with doodled stars
scattered across your bedroom floor

I play-play-played those dented drums
(cast-off cake tins of your mum's)
accompanied by the pick and strum
of your wreck-necked red guitar
And we knew we'd go far,
we were dizzy with it

You taped it all on your dad's reel-to-reel:
my unsure voice, your backing hum,
the dum-dum-thrum
of those battered drums,
and the slip-slide-scratch of six steel strings

We'd sprawl out on the carpet when
the DJ revealed the new top ten,
your Bolan hair a crazy tangle
and my hipster pale-sky jeans
embroidered with our rockstar dreams

Mandy Huggins's travel writing and short fiction has been placed and shortlisted in numerous writing competitions, including Bare Fiction, Ink Tears, Words with Jam, Fish, and Bradt Travel Guides. She won the BGTW New Travel Writer Award 2014 and was runner-up in the 2016 Dragonfly Tea Short Story Prize.

http://troutiemcfishtales.blogspot.co.uk

Wolves Chew Through Chains Like They Do Prey

Nina S. Stone

They say:
Start acting like a lady.
Stop pushing away.
Smile more.
Be more delicate with your actions,
your words, that body of yours.
They warn: You will end up alone.
Her answer: a smile, cutting
Teeth, dangerous edges
Lipstick, bright,
(the color of the blood she shares with wolves)
Her everything, a roughly sharpened warning
"I'm already alone,"

I'm **Nina S Stone**, a 20 year old student. I'm the possibilities glinting in stars, I'm a written word, I'm the huge small gestures and kind words from strangers. I'm the sincerity of friends whose presence rivals the universe. All that I love that step by step makes me who I am.

http://thekingsleepsstill.tumblr.com

Hard Labour

Janis Clark

That day, time hung draped in
corners like a cloak discarded.

The clock's hands circled its face
thirty times. Three rush hours came

and went while lives sped on beyond this
room of monitors and dials showing

your tiny heart still beating strong within
my weakening body - defeated at the final mile.

Janis Clark lives in Drumnadrochit, near Inverness. Her poems are published in various magazines and anthologies and she has been commended in a number of poetry competitions.

Twitter: @frogfeet50

Once I was a Tree

Nicola Warwick

Once I was a tree that bent in the wind
and you must have thought
my trunk would snap
before you needed to speak.

Autumn came. I wept leaves
into the water and bore no fruit.
My blossom had been barren.

I passed winter in cold and silence,
branches hacked to a stark silhouette
of black and torpor. I was a pollard.
Frost kept me warm.

Spring followed with a rush
of rains and damage. Deep in my roots
came a change – leaf buds burst
from barren knots and my heartwood throbbed.

Nina Wawick lives in Suffolk and works in local government. She has had work in several poetry magazines and been commended or won prizes in competitions. Her first poetry collection, Groundings, was published by Cinnamon Press in 2014. She is studying for an MA in Creative Writing with the Open University.

Twitter: @warwick_nicola

The Light is Different

Eithne Cullen

The light is different here, they told her.

And she knew that they were right.

From the moment she stepped off the plane,
hit by a wall of shard-sharp clarity,
her eyes adjusted to the glowing haze.

She took her palm-sized pad of paints
out into that light and captured clear lines of buildings,
shadows cast by towers and trees,
lines on the faces of fellow gazers
glints of icy white in beggars' eyes.
And in the sky a sinking blush of sun,
the tricky water's shades of white and blue.

Homeward the Central Line took her
from tunnel-dark to squalid half-light.
The Stratford shoppers' neon lighted shrine,
streetlights barely picking out the shapes
of rows of terraced houses and tumbled graves.

The light was different here, she told herself.

She put her paints away.

Eithne Cullen was born in Dublin and moved to London when she was six years old. She writes stories and poems. She lives with her husband in East London. She is unashamedly proud of her three grown up children, and endeavours to embarrass them as often as she can.

Garden Gate

Jennifer Hunt

I always wanted a washing line
along the path to the garden gate
a wooden post at either end
a rope slung in between.
I imagined our wet clothes
hung out to dry in the westerly wind
tangling together,
his shirts, my smock,
trapped but weightless in the air,
towels, tethered by wooden pegs,
trying to take off in the threadbare light.
Our sheets would bleach
to rain-washed white
and I would stand
arms upstretched
hair blowing in my eyes
as I edge along the path
towards the gate
which would swing open
to the sloping fenceless fields beyond.

Mother of four and grandmother of eight, **Jennifer Hunt** wrote her first poem in her Mother Goose book aged six. She has an MA (with distinction) in Creative Writing from Bath Spa and runs a weekly writing workshop. She has been successful in several poetry competitions and is also an artist.

www.seashed.co.uk

Two Inches Numb

Lee Nash

You would think that if someone
witnessed a body issue from your flesh
a being their own seed had set
that if they watched the knife score the living marble
if breathing fast under their hospital mask
they saw you cleaved in two
if sitting beside the green curtain erected over your chest
they peered into the rendered belly
if their arms held a person's first attitude
not once but twice
that this someone would never leave
but like that surgeon and his team of medics
you never saw them again
were left with a strange wrenching sensation in your gut
nothing to anaesthetise the strain
a pair of scars faint as a double moonbow
all cords cut
all memories fading like a linea nigra
two lives to raise
two inches numb above your pubic bone

A poet, editor, musician and mother, **Lee Nash** lives in the Charente department, France. She is in the process of collating poems for her first collection (life reflections and sketches from her travels so far) and two pamphlets, one eco-poetry and the other in praise of her female heroes.

leenashpoetry.com

A Young Man Once

Barney Harper

Small man,
once tall in policeman's blue, eyes
now milky, blood-rimmed,
half-blind.
I am my father behind him in the mirror,
my sister from a distance.
His body now bent
towards hazardous ground:
the tops of curbs
and stick-searched dips
that trip. He misses
the sky's gifts
of cotton strewn canopies,
azurean panoplies,
now swapped for asphalt
and the tips of his own black shoes.

Barney Harper first got noticed as a writer at age 12 when she won an essay competition for her piece on the unparalleled joy of a good burger. She was awarded a meal with her headmistress (which didn't include a burger). She is still waiting for her second major literary prize.

Website: barneywritenow.wordpress.com

Nativity

Lindy Newns

I was the chosen one.
I walked across the room, did not acknowledge
by a grin my classmates' giggles.
I was above it all - somewhere in a dream
where people watched and were amazed
that I - noisy, bossy, kisser of boys -
could capture so well the serene composure
of Holy Mary, full of grace and silent
on her tiny feet. I ponder it in my heart.

I have no memory of the play itself
except that Richard Lees was Joseph.
Or a camel. And that is all.
Oh – and that my mum had to provide
my costume and the length of blue velvet
left her short of cash for a month,
so we had to do without our Angel Delight.

Lindy Newns is an award winning playwright who downsized to poetry when her teaching career ate her life. Commended in the Portico Poetry competition 2014, she has had poems published in Orbis and elsewhere. She wishes she could rap like some of the poets in Manchester's Young Identity. Maybe in another life, of which she's had several, but there's always room for another.

?

Short Stories

The short story category was for entries of up to 2,000 words, not including the title. The short story genre is a staple of writing competitions the world over and many writers will hone their skills in this medium before venturing into the world of longer fiction.

In some ways, writing short fiction is much harder than writing longer pieces, this is because the writer doesn't have the luxury of space and time to expand on a theme or introduce too many layers. Most short stories seem to work best when they consider a single perspective or a specific event.

Advice from our short story judges

Carol Warham

https://carolwarham.blogspot.co.uk/

It was a privilege to be asked to judge the Hysteria Short Story competition and I thoroughly enjoyed doing it. Many congratulations to all who entered and especially to those who made the short lists. It was a great achievement.

I estimated I read about 100 stories and how different they all were. I felt writing some of the stories had been very cathartic for their authors. It seemed as if they were opening out onto the paper and describing their own problems and struggles, rather than writing a story.

One thing I particularly noticed was that there was a distinct lack of checking and polishing the entries before they were submitted. Mistakes in punctuation, grammar and spelling were often glaring. It was a shame as this could and did spoil the enjoyment of reading the story.

It is always worthwhile having an opening that is going to hook the reader, and make them want to read more. Occasionally, some stories started off in a very mundane manner and I felt the first paragraph could have been deleted as the 'real' story started further down the page.

I really appreciated the entries that were a little 'quirky' or humorous. When entering a competition it certainly pays to try and think of a subject a little different from the run of the mill. The reader wants to be entertained, to feel something, even if it's bringing a lump to the throat.

I would also advise once you have finished writing your story, read it out loud. This does help to show you areas where the writing style is clunky, the dialogue doesn't sound natural or the punctuation is incorrect.

Having said that, the main criteria are to enjoy what you do and get satisfaction from it. So, keep writing and good luck with the next competition.

Catherine Menon

cgmenon.wordpress.com

Firstly, make sure that your first paragraph really gets a reader's attention. It doesn't need to be flashy or filled with action; a descriptive paragraph can also work. But this is your first chance to stand out from the crowd, so do make use of it.

Your story should also have an overall arc - beginning, middle and end. It's important for there to be some movement in the story and for the main character to undergo some sort of change. Again, this doesn't need to be drastic. It could be as simple as changing their mind about something, or understanding a situation they previously didn't.

Finally, make sure the story tidies up the loose ends! You can certainly leave quite a lot that's ambiguous, but there has to be some sense of resolution.

Pat Good

Before I enter a competition I either print out the rules or note down the main points for consideration. Knowing my entry meets the competition requirements means I'm confident that it's going to pass the preliminary checks and go through to the judging stage.

When I finish writing I read my work out loud. Hearing the words mean I pick up on any bit that doesn't flow. This lets me check the length of sentences, choice of verbs and adverbs, and catch repetitive words or phrases.

I try to complete my entry a week or two (not always easy) before the deadline. If I manage this I put my writing away and when I revisit it I see it with fresh eyes and can give it a final polish before letting it go.

I enjoy reading writing tips and hope someone out there will find these ones useful.

Finally, I'd like to say that the majority of the stories I had the pleasure of reading in the competition were diverse, well written and entertaining. If your story wasn't placed remember it may still find success elsewhere. So please keep writing – there's always Hysteria 2017 to aim for.

Anne Wilson

www.authoranne.co.uk

One thing I noticed was lack of structure. Several entries lacked a narrative arc of beginning, middle and end. This is the journey the reader embarks on when they invest their time in reading a story and I think this is where to put 'creative' into creative writing.

Some writers relate an incident or experience exactly in the manner in which it unfolded and this is a record of events more suited to article writing, journalism or memoir. Even if you are writing from life, your story still needs to be just that, a story. It needs to be woven imaginatively or given a twist; perhaps asking yourself 'what if' or 'what might have happened a little differently?' in order to achieve a satisfactory ending. The inspiration can come from real life but this is a story so doesn't have to be true, unless of course it is hugely entertaining in its own right.

Embed a narrative hook at the beginning to make the reader want to know what happens and endow your characters with as much individuality as you can, being careful not to stereotype them.

Treat each non-placement as an opportunity to improve your story in some way.

Hannah Onoguwe

www.instagram.com/hannahonoguwe

Being asked to judge entries for the Hysteria 2016 writing competition was a privilege. It was also humbling as it alerted me to those things that illuminate a writer's work, which I admit I am often blind to in my own writing. Things like an authentic character whose voice was as clear as my best friend's with its attending quirks and opinions. It was also important that the stories didn't try to cram too much into the plot because that felt like being forced to go through

The Lord of the Rings in half an hour. Inevitably, I felt little to no connection with the characters.

Stories that resonated with me captured emotions well, enabling me to laugh, empathize, or roll my eyes with or at the characters. They also contained fresh and unique descriptions, although here some caution is necessary: simple is best. Those that tried too hard were often long-winded and lost me. Other stories contained a surprise ending, not necessarily a twist, but one which showed the character changed in some believable way. I didn't have to love the characters, but I could respect them and their choices.

Marcia Woolf

www.marciawoolf.com

On a practical level, make sure that you have spell-checked your story and been through it carefully for typos, errors of punctuation and grammar, and repeated use of the same word or phrase. Can any sentences or phrases be misinterpreted? Are there any unintentional howlers? If possible, get a keen-eyed friend or colleague to read it as well. Use a clear typeface/font and standard layout, and remember to stick to the word count. Even the best stories can be let down by mangled syntax, mixed metaphors and poor presentation, so I would always advise finding a little time for a final polish to ensure that your work really stands out.

A 'TA-DA' Moment

Sandra Crook

"You were never really on board with the plan, were you?"

Ruth is nothing if not direct. My daughter-in-law and I haven't enjoyed a close relationship, but there's always been a healthy respect between us, and we cut each other a lot of slack. She is, as usual, correct in her assumption.

"Being consulted might have gone a long way towards smoothing the path," I remark acidly, even now, after all this time.

"I said they should have waited till you came back."

I believe her.

She places the last of my ornaments in the packing case. "Is that everything now?"

"That's it," I say, looking around.

A chapter is coming to an end.

It's funny how life trundles on, day after day, the same old routine and then suddenly it swerves dramatically off the old familiar path. I remember the shock of that moment, even now.

I'd been away for a month, visiting my sister who'd just come out of hospital. As I turned into our road, I'd been stunned to see a "Sold" sign outside my own home.

"I hope you gave someone a rocket for that," I observed, setting down my case and pecking Joe on the cheek. "Who's selling up? I thought everyone round here was rooted in concrete."

"I'll make a cuppa, love," muttered Joe. "We need to have a little chat."

It hadn't been an estate agent's mistake. Joe had been sheepish, defensive, but determined as he'd unfurled his plan. His plan. Not mine. It had been assumed, by both Joe and our son Greg, that I'd go along with it. The estate agent had jumped the gun, it seemed, before they'd had a chance to discuss it with me.

"Our Greg needs to get started, Ellie, surely you see that? Him and Ruth. They need a proper home, not that cramped council flat. Our grandkids need a garden, space to play."

"Of course they do, but what's that got to do with selling our house?"

"Look," and his tone had become painstakingly patronising, "our house will go to them in the end anyway. But this way they get the benefit early, right when they need it most. We sell up, they use the money from the sale to buy a house. Greg will build an extension on that house, a granny flat for us. It's perfect, don't you agree? They've already found a house, and I've seen the plans for the extension. We'll be separate from them, our own front door and everything, but we'll still be there for them. You can look after the kids when they come home from school, just like you do now, we can babysit without having to trail over the other side of town, and best of all..."

He'd paused for effect. I could recognise a 'ta-da' moment when I saw one.

He continued triumphantly, "... they'll be on hand to look after us when we need care."

Now that truly was a 'ta-da' moment.

"Care...?" My voice rose an octave, and I'd steadied myself with a deep breath. Joe was staring at me.

"And where do we live while they're building the extension?" I asked, watching his shoulders relax slightly, as he construed my question as the first step towards acceptance.

"I've found a few park homes for us to look at. Nice places, with a bit of a garden so you can still have the grandkids round after school. They're available for rent for a twelve-month period, by which time the extension should be completed. And if construction runs on a bit, we can extend by six months if necessary."

"You want us to move from here and live in a caravan?" Now I really was screeching.

"Oh, look Ellie, these park homes aren't caravans nowadays. They're quite luxurious, loads of old folk are buying them, freeing up capital so that the young ones can get started. There'll be quite a community spirit there, you'll see."

Old folks...? Who's that then?

The bickering continued.

And Joe turned to censure.

"You're being self-centred, Ellie. Young people need to get a foot-hold in life. And we can make that possible for them, whilst they're still young enough to enjoy it."

"I know all that," I protested, though I briefly wondered who had given us a 'foothold in life'. "And if I'd been involved from the beginning maybe I'd have felt differently. But you've all worked behind my back, without a thought for my feelings."

Time now for hurt disappointment on Joe's part.

"I suppose I just assumed you'd want the best for them, Ellie. Maybe I shouldn't have taken that for granted, but I thought I knew you well enough."

"If you knew me well enough, you'd have realised I'd hate having this sprung on me without consultation."

Over the next few days it seemed every turn in the conversation brought us to confrontation. Things were very uncomfortable when Greg and Ruth visited, and I noticed my daughter-in-law nudging Joe out into the garden for a private word.

After that Joe switched back to a defensive approach.

"We just went to investigate the position with the estate agent. The buyers were in the area at the time, looking for a detached house. The agent arranged a viewing that same day, just to confirm it was the kind of house they were after. And they loved it. I did ask the agent not to put the sign up until I'd spoken to you, but you know what they're like..."

And that, it seemed, was that.

In the days that followed, I'd sensed I was being watched, talked about. It was unnerving to feel like a particularly undesirable fly in the ointment, and it was uncomfortable, feeling selfish, when all I'd really wanted was to be consulted. Or was that true? Was that all I wanted?

There must have been a 'euphoric' period, as the three of them fleshed out the project. There'd have been stages when Greg and Ruth were in turn incredulous, then grateful, then excited as the plans took shape. But I'd missed out on all that. By the time I got involved, it was signed, sealed and delivered. Everyone was knee-deep in practicalities, and I was up to my neck in resentment.

The house sale went through quickly. Far too quickly. Moving house is stressful. Moving from a house you've lived in for thirty years is really hard work. But moving house when you're simply not committed to the idea is practically impossible. I tried my best though, once I was over the initial shock and outrage. And I must have been convincing enough.

"I'm glad you've seen it our way, Ellie," said Joe one night, gripping my hand and shaking it gently, "you had us all worried there for a bit."

There it was again... 'you' and 'us'... 'your' and 'our'.

"You're a brick, Ma," said Greg, "you'll never know how much we appreciate this. And I'll get the extension built quickly so you're not in the park home for long. It'll be great having you so close. I know you love having the kids after school, and this way you'll see them all the time. Ruth can get a proper job, now she won't have to take time off for school holidays. We really should have done this sooner."

My fixed smile, the one I painted on each morning, and peeled off every night, must have calcified into a rictus grin. I did love having the children after school, but it was equally lovely during school holidays when Ruth took time off work to look after them. I felt most 'ungranny-like', but I didn't want to spend my life in the role of permanent baby-sitter.

It was the kids though, and only the kids, that kept me focused, ensuring I stayed 'on song' over the following months.

"Awww Gran, we'll each have our own bedroom. And there'll be a garden, and we're going to have swings and seesaws. It'll be terrific, really mega. And you'll be there all the time, so we can get a dog and maybe a rabbit, because when we go on holiday, you can look after them ... and you can drive us to scouts and swimming and dancing... "

Their joy was infectious and I'd loved it. Their schedule for the remainder of my life was rather less appealing.

"Is that everything then?" Ruth repeats, glancing around the cramped space I've called home for the last twelve months since the house was sold.

"I've everything I need," I say. "There's not a lot of room on a narrow-boat."

She takes hold of my hand.

"Are you sure about this, Mum? It's a big step, you know."

I think that's the first time she's called me Mum. I realise that in all the time I've known her, she's never added a name tag in conversations, not even my Christian name. Perhaps that omission lent a mutually comfortable distance. But we've become closer recently. We've learned things we never knew about each other – such as the fact that her parents often took narrow-boating holidays – as did mine. We share a passionate interest in boats, and Ruth even came with me to look at the one I've bought, and she's going to help me move it to a base closer to home. Their home. Theirs and Joe's.

I smile at her.

"I'm sure, Ruth. Never more so."

I don't mention the second thoughts I've had along the way. I'd saved a small nest egg for a rainy day, but when my sister died a few months ago, the fact of my own mortality really came home to me, pushing me onward. And the few thousand she left me in her will helped me realise the dream.

Joe isn't here. He's working with Greg on the extension at their new house. Twelve months down the line, the work has only just started, and I suspect it might never have started at all if I hadn't sprung my plans on them. I think they imagined I'd change my mind if they got a move on, but it won't work. My son and husband have been incredulous, angry and resentful in turn. I've been accused, once again, of being selfish. Maybe I am.

Joe's been hurt, but I'm hopeful he'll get over it, so that we can remain friends. And he'll be well looked after, living in the grandad-flat with everyone close by, giving assistance when he needs it.

Ruth sits back on her heels, staring at me. "You're a tough cookie, aren't you?"

Am I? You can go on, day after day in the same old routine, and suddenly something triggers a deviation. You may have engineered it yourself, but more often than not, someone or something else is the catalyst. We tend to drift inexorably into the compulsion to maintain and nurture the status quo. But once change begins to disturb the equilibrium, the need for more change just seems to grow exponentially. There's a kind of 'ta-da' moment.

I'm sure I'll miss them all, and I hope they'll make me welcome when I visit, which I hope to do regularly.

But I've been anchored for too long, bobbing around on the waters of life, allowing everything to happen around me.

Now I've realised there's a whole new world to discover out there. And time is in short supply.

"Will you rename the boat?" asks Ruth, shoving the packing cases towards the door with her foot. "It's supposed to be bad luck, but personally I'd find it hard to live with 'Serendipity' for very long."

"I think I might," I say, "I've got a few ideas floating around in my head."

"How about 'Phoenix' then?" She grins at me.

I smile. "Nice one, but I think I've got something in mind."

I look round the tiny lounge one last time.

I'm going to name the boat 'Ta-Da'.

Sandra Crook, a former Human Resources Manager from Dorset, UK, now cruises the French waterways in a Dutch barge several months of the year. A number of her short stories, flash fiction pieces and articles have been published in magazines, newspapers and anthologies. She's recently enjoyed several competition successes.

https://castelsarrasin.wordpress.com

Safe as Houses

Christine Griffin

Friday morning 6.30 am

The police let us come back last night, but we've hardly slept since then. Now in the early dawn Mike and I stand clutching our coffee cups, trying to blot out the noise from the street. The curtains are drawn and the doors are all locked. We can hear them in our garden and someone is banging on the back door yelling our names. As if we hadn't been through enough.

And I don't care what Mike says. There's no way I'm staying in this place any longer than I have to.

The previous Tuesday morning 3.40 am

I'm floating somewhere between a high mountain and an icy fjord. I ought to be frightened but I'm not. I can hear something and I'm searching the desolate landscape below to see where the noise is coming from. There's no sign of life anywhere but I can hear it, faint but unmistakable. It's the sound of a baby crying. Not a hungry cry or a tired cry. It's a cry of abandonment howling in desolation in the icy wind.

I jump awake, pouring with sweat, my heart beating. The clock shows 3.41 and Mike is snoring softly beside me. They warned me about these nightmares. It'll take a while to get over it, they said. Well it's four months now and if anything the dreams are worse. And always I can hear her – I never doubted it would be a girl – wailing somewhere in outer darkness.

It was because of her that we'd moved into this house. I disliked it on first sight but Mike had promised me that he'd turn it into a palace.

Something to get his teeth into, he said. But so far the only thing he's got his teeth into is the cellar which he's turning into a music studio. The cellar gives me the creeps so I hardly ever go down there. Mike spends every evening and most weekends hammering and drilling while I sit in the miserable lounge pretending to watch television.

Two weeks after we moved here, she decided to leave the world she'd never even lived in. They told me it wasn't my fault, but of course it was. All that lifting, not to mention the anxiety of the move. And the thing is I'd been really happy in the old house. I've never been a fan of big houses and there would have been plenty of room for the three of us where we were. And the old neighbours had been lovely. Mrs Matthews from next door had wept when we moved out. Here, no-one speaks to you. On the one side is a young couple. I've never even spoken to them. I have no idea who lives on the other side. Sometimes I see a man coming and going carrying bags of shopping, but I never see anyone else.

At 3.56, I give up and go downstairs to make some tea. The kitchen looks grim under the fluorescent strip-light. As I sip the tea, I brace myself mentally for the coming day. It's Tuesday, the day the miscarriage support group meets. Every Tuesday I vow I will go but when it comes to it I never do. Today though will be different. I'm going to wash my hair, put on some make-up and walk into that room full of other abandoned nearly- mothers.

I will. I'll do it.

7.46 am

Mike and I sit at the breakfast bar, trying to make conversation. He looks tired, despite having slept the night through.

'You up in the night again?' he says.

'Yeah. The usual stuff.'

'Listen, Karen. They told you not to do that. You just get into the habit.'

'I know. I really try not to.' I pause, not wanting to meet his eye. 'Anyway today's going to be different. I've decided I'm going to that Support Group thing.'

'You said that last week. And the week before.'

'Yes, well I mean it this time.'

He chews his toast and stares at the floor. 'Last night,' he says then stops.

'What about last night?'

'When I was putting in the supports for the speakers.'

Normally I zone out when he starts on about his sound systems, but there's something different in his tone this time.

'Mike. What about last night? What are you trying to say?'

'Well I thought I heard it too. That crying you hear in your nightmares.' My piece of toast slips from my fingers. 'Like it's lost or something.'

He pauses, looking straight at me.

'Like she's lost.'

There's no mistaking the emphasis on the 'she'. This is the first time he's been able to say anything at all about her and I feel the tears well up. Maybe I won't go to the meeting today after all. I don't want to make a fool of myself.

9.20 am

I take the new scarf out of the drawer and knot it round my neck. My hair is neat and my make-up in place. The meeting starts at ten and I scrabble about for my keys, anxious to get outside before I lose my nerve.

The sound of the doorbell jangles through the house and I freeze. Who would be calling at this time? It's too early for the post and I don't know anyone else.

If people are animals then the man on my doorstop is a bull, angry and pacing. He puts his face right up to mine and I can smell his foul breath.

'I've got a message for that bloke of yours. Tell him to stop his bloody drilling or else.'

'I'm sorry,' I say. 'Who are you?'

'I'm from next door and I'm getting very, very upset about the racket he makes every night. Tell him if it doesn't stop, he'll know about it.' He opens his donkey jacket and I see the knuckle duster quite clearly. There's no doubting his intention.

I don't go to my meeting that morning.

11.28 am

My third cup of coffee has gone cold as I sit wondering whether to call Mike. He hates it when I ring him at work, but that horrible man has left me shaking uncontrollably. I'm fiddling with my phone, my fingers hovering over his number, when I hear it. A baby and its desperate crying. Normally it underscores my nightmares, but this time I'm very much awake. The sound is coming from the hallway – I'm convinced of it. I move towards the kitchen door, my pulse banging in my ears.

The hallway is empty of course, and the sound has stopped. There's a thump as the mail lands on the mat and at exactly the same time the crying starts again. This time there's no doubt about where it's coming from.

It's coming from the cellar.

Mike's made loads of progress since I was down here last. He's fixed up his sound desk and there are speakers on the wall and some microphones placed around the room. David Bowie and the Rolling Stones glower from the walls and his huge record selection is stacked high.   Various headsets hang from hooks around the walls. He's left some of the equipment switched on and the speakers round the room are hissing and crackling.

But that's all the noise there is. Apart from that, the cellar is silent. Absolutely no sound of a baby crying. I'm just about to go back upstairs when I hear a faint male voice echoing round the room. It's indistinct but I can't help thinking it's the same voice as the angry man who had stood on my doorstep earlier that morning. I realise it's coming from one of the speakers and I fiddle round until I find the volume button. The sound rises and I hear another noise now, a bit like an animal grunting. The man raises his voice, the animal grunts and squeals louder and then a baby starts crying. Only this time it's not in my nightmares – it's very real and as far as I can tell, it's coming from the cellar next door.

2.15

They've evacuated our street because armed police are surrounding the house next door. We're sitting in a room in the police station, trying to take in everything we've been told. A fortified cellar, they're saying. And it wasn't an animal I heard, but a young girl thirteen years old, kept prisoner by her father. It seems she's been down there for the whole of her life.

And there's a baby. My mind skitters away from that dreadful thought.

Mike keeps saying the same thing over and over, as if focusing on that stops him thinking about anything else.

'I never leave my stuff switched on. Never. Why did I do that? I never leave it on.'

The policewoman sitting with us nods.

'Just think if I hadn't. Anything might have happened to that poor girl. And right next to us as well. '

'I'm afraid just about everything has already happened to the poor girl.' The policewoman is amazingly calm considering the horror of what's unfolding before us. 'From what we can gather, he only ever spoke to her when absolutely necessary, so she's never learned to speak. Karen, you heard the noises. That's how she communicated.'

'But the baby?' Mike asks. 'I don't understand.'

But I understand. I'm ahead of him on this so I'm not surprised at the policewoman's next words. I reach for his hand.

'Well, there'll be tests of course, but it's almost certainly his.'

He stares at her in horror. 'The father's you mean? '

'I'm afraid so.'

'But why didn't anyone know? Didn't she have a mother? How could people not know?'

The policewoman looks away, her face grim. 'You'd be surprised what people get away with. It's easier than you might think to live beneath the radar. I should know. There's not much I haven't seen in this job. Our team will be looking into what happened to the girl's mother but their priority at the moment is to get that child and the baby into a safe environment.'

How can they possibly know where to start, I think. The poor thing can't even speak.

As if reading my mind, the policewoman touches my arm. 'We have some wonderful people who know how to deal with this situation. She isn't the first and sadly she won't be the last.'

Two months later

The reporters lost interest fairly quickly and after several days of harassment, they decided to leave us alone. We know nothing about what has happened to the girl and her baby. As for her so-called father, we can only assume that they've hidden him away until the case comes to court. We've given our witness statements and that will be it until the trial. None of our business any more.

What is our business now is getting our lives back on an even keel. There was no way we could have stayed in this house after what happened. . All his equipment is boxed up in the hallway and the cellar door is locked. This afternoon we're moving into a rental property thanks to a tip-off from our old neighbour. It's a few doors away from her and I can't wait to leave here. It's small and cosy with a little bit of garden. A south facing garden so it gets the sun most of the day. And no cellar.

I never did get to my support group. Doesn't seem much point now. There's my ante-natal classes to go to and the back bedroom in the new place to sort out. I'm hedging my bets this time and going for yellow.

The doorbell rings and Mike lets in the removal men. 'Leave it all to us,' says one of them, winking at me.

'Oh, don't worry, 'I say. 'This time I'm not lifting so much as a finger.'

Christine Griffin lives in Gloucestershire and is a member of several writing groups which provide her with great stimulus and support. She has been published both locally and nationally and regularly reads her work on local radio. She recently performed some of her work at the Cheltenham Literature Festival.

When Jesus Came To Tea

Olga Wojtas

I was checking Ben's schoolbag and Ben was eating his cornflakes. Or rather, he was lifting his spoon and tilting it so that the milk dripped back into the bowl.

Gordon cleared his throat warningly.

"I'm thinking," said Ben. "What kind of biscuits would Jesus like?"

He looked at me, and I realised he actually wanted an answer.

"I think Jesus would like any kind of biscuit."

"But what kind would be his most favourite?"

I wasn't used to such a philosophical question so early in the morning, but I felt it was important to encourage this new interest.

"Well, he always paid attention to the things other people didn't bother with, didn't he, so I suppose it would be those pink wafer biscuits that always get left at the bottom of the tin."

"Then could you get in some pink wafer biscuits cos I've invited him for tea."

"You've invited Jesus for tea?" asked Gordon. "That's a pretty impressive imaginary friend you've got."

Ben let the spoon clatter into the cereal bowl. "He's not a maginary friend! He's in my class."

Gordon and I exchanged glances. Sometimes we worried about whether our son was a wee bit too precocious.

"He's new," Ben went on. "I said he could come for tea after football practice on Thursday."

"I thought Jesus had a long beard and sandals," said Gordon. "Sandals can't be very practical for football."

"He's eight," said Ben witheringly. "He hasn't got a beard. And he wears football boots."

Enlightenment was beginning to dawn.

"Is he Spanish? Or South American?" I asked. "It's spelled 'Jesus,' but it's pronounced 'Hay-zoos'."

"He's called Jesus," said Ben firmly.

"Where's he from?" I persisted.

"Nazareth," said Gordon. "Everybody knows that."

I gave up. Eventually, I managed to get them both out of the house, having instructed Ben to ask Jesus to ask his mum to ring me. And then I got on with my latest commission, hand-made paper with mimosa and rose petals. It was turning out beautifully, perfect wedding stationery. The happy couple would be delighted. And that always made me feel a little bit sad.

Gordon and I had been together for twelve years now. I loved him as much as ever, if not more, with his ghastly jokes, and his terrible DIY, and his utter devotion to Ben and me. But he didn't believe in marriage. On the anniversary of us moving in together, he gave me a card of two bluebirds. Inside he'd written the words of a Joni Mitchell song: "We don't need no piece of paper from the city hall, keeping us tied and true."

I thought it was romantic. But I thought we'd get married when I got pregnant, which we didn't. Then I thought we'd get definitely married after Ben was born, which we didn't.

Gordon didn't think it mattered. But more and more, I felt it did. Especially now Ben was at primary school. Of course there were all sorts of non-traditional family units. But I didn't like the fact that Ben and Gordon shared a surname, and I didn't. Gordon and I always turned up together at parents' events, but I worried that the teachers might think Gordon had custody of his wife's child, or had adopted my son.

At one point, I suggested hyphenating our names together.

"Wow, that's a fantastic idea!" said Gordon. "And you know what would be even better? Changing our names to Ponsonby-Smythe at the same time."

I took that as a no.

I had just finished lifting the stacks of paper out of the mould when the phone rang.

It was a woman's voice, foreign, pleasant. She said her name, but I couldn't make it out, and then she said: "I'm Jesus's mother."

Jesus, not Hay-zoos. She obviously reckoned Brits couldn't cope with foreign pronunciations.

I introduced myself as Becky, Ben's mum, which avoided the surname problem, and then I decided to do my bit for international relations. "I can make paella or fajitas or something like that if that's what he prefers to eat."

But Mrs Indistinct assured me that he would eat whatever was put in front of him, and I was no further forward as to whether he came from Madrid or Buenos Aires.

Ben decided that he wanted his favourite, spag bol, and reminded me again about the pink biscuits.

"He's making a big deal of this," I said to Gordon later. "He's bringing home one of his school mates, the way he does all the time, but he obviously feels there's something special about him."

"Well, that'll be a first for a mate of Ben's if he's not a very naughty boy. Maybe he IS the Messiah."

I spent most of Thursday working on the wedding stationery commission, and then had a mad dash to make the flat look respectable. I was doing some unaccustomed dusting in the sitting room when I found Ben's goldfish floating dead at the top of its bowl. I had never exactly bonded with Goldie, who seemed to me to have limited entertainment value, but I knew Ben would be devastated. I was about to consign Goldie to a watery grave in the loo when the bride-to-be rang to discuss the wedding paper for the third time that week.

I'd only just managed to get rid of her when the front door opened.

"This is Jesus," said Ben, with an air of proprietorial pride.

Jesus was a small, olive-skinned child with jet black hair. He put out his hand to shake mine. I was completely taken aback by this level of politeness. Usually, when Ben's friends met me, they kept their heads down and edged past as though I was the Wicked Witch of the West, and I suspected Ben did much the same with his friends' parents.

"Hello, Jesus. Very nice to meet you," I said, shaking hands.

"Hello, Mrs Craig."

"She's not Mrs Craig, she's Ms Barry," Ben intervened. "My mum and dad aren't married."

I cringed inwardly. Jesus undoubtedly came from a traditional background, and what was he going to think of me now? I couldn't even take refuge in "Call me Becky" since I was sure he hadn't been brought up to call adults by their first names.

But he was smiling at me as though as I was his favourite person in the whole world. "It's very nice to meet you, Ms Barry."

I went to get them a drink before tea, and when I came back, I found them standing by the goldfish bowl. My first thought was that Jesus was going to tell his parents about a woman living in sin whose flat was littered with the corpses of household pets. My second thought was how upset Ben was going to be.

And then I realised Ben wasn't upset at all. He was laughing and joking with Jesus as they watched the late Goldie swimming round and round the bowl.

"Tea in five minutes," I said faintly.

Jesus had impeccable table manners. There was a stillness and a maturity about him, but also a sense of fun, with that ready smile and those shining brown eyes.

"Where are you from, Jesus?" I asked.

"Montague Street," he said.

"No, I mean, before you came here."

"We were in Glasgow for a few months."

After they had finished eating, they went to play in Ben's room. When I walked past the open door some time later, that only confirmed things. Play normally consisted of Ben and his mates jumping on and off the bed pretending to be pirates. But Jesus was sitting cross-legged on the bed while Ben sat quietly on the floor listening to him.

I grabbed Gordon as soon as he got home, and pulled him into the kitchen for a private conversation.

"Okay," said Gordon, "let's see if I've got this right. You think this small boy is Jesus because he won't tell you where he's from, he doesn't eat with his mouth open, and he shook hands with you?"

"How do you explain Goldie?"

"Ah yes. Yea, he hath raised Goldie from the dead. Love, I don't want to sound like a Doubting Thomas, but have you considered that Goldie wasn't dead, but only sleeping?"

"That fish was visibly decomposing," I said.

"Then it sounds like a really great miracle, but you know what would really impress me? Give him a jug of water and see if he can turn it into Rioja."

"You're not taking this seriously. There's something really different about him. You know what Ben and his mates are usually like, creating havoc. But Ben's just been sitting at his feet while Jesus tells him a story."

"I think you'll find it's called a parable," said Gordon. "Like 'Don't hide your light under a bushel or the bushel will catch fire.'"

"And when I brought out the plate of biscuits, he immediately took the pink wafer."

"Well, you should have said that to start with," said Gordon. "Verily, that is conclusive proof. Tell me, are you using any new substances in your paper-making? Maybe you shouldn't breathe in so deeply."

I rolled my eyes at him. "It's time you took him home. You'll see. There's something very special about that boy."

Jesus shook hands with Gordon, shook hands with me, complimented me on my cooking, and thanked me for a lovely evening. I was gratified to see Gordon look quite startled. After they'd left, I asked Ben what he and Jesus had been talking about.

He shrugged. "Dunno. Stuff."

"Did he tell you about his father?"

"S'pose."

"What did he say?"

"Dunno."

"You can invite him round any time, you know."

"Can I go online before I go to bed?"

"No, go and brush your teeth."

Gordon seemed thoughtful when he got home. "It was the weirdest thing," he said. "The car cut out totally on the way there, right in the middle of the road. Lucky there was nobody behind us. I turned the key a few times, but not a thing. I was just about to ring the AA when Jesus told me to try again. His voice, there was something - he was really calm, really confident. So I tried again and it was fine. Maybe I should take it into the garage to get it checked out."

"Or maybe you don't need to," I said as I dished up the spag bol. "So what about his parents?"

Gordon hadn't seen a nameplate on the front door and, like me, he hadn't been able to make out what their name was when they told him. They had invited him in, but he hadn't seen any other clues. Perhaps they didn't have anything distinctive from their homeland or perhaps Gordon was being his usual unobservant self.

But he had been observant about something. At the end of our meal, he insisted that I go and sit on the sofa while he cleared up and made me a coffee.

He came and sat beside me, putting his arm round me. "They were great, you know? A great couple. A great family. You could tell they all really cared about one another."

I snuggled into him and he kissed the top of my head. "You know I love you," he said. "You know that, don't you?"

"I know," I said.

He took a breath. I could tell he was going to ask something else. I waited for his question, the last miracle of the day.

"Are there any of those pink biscuits left?" he said.

Olga Wojtas is half-Scottish and half-Polish, a journalist by day and a creative writer by night. She lives in Edinburgh where she attended the school which inspired Muriel Spark's "The Prime of Miss Jean Brodie." She dreams of becoming the crème de la crème.

Twitter: @OlgaWojtas

Inspiration

Linda Fawke

It was the piece of cardboard with 'Birmingham' scrawled on it. It pulled me like a magnet. Then he was in the car, sitting beside me, smelling of rain and wet wool, my haven of dryness splashed with mud and relief.

No sensible woman picks up a hitch-hiker. I never did. But I had now. Yes, I'd told him. I was heading for Brum. Yes, I'd said, no problem to drop him off on the outskirts. I pulled back on to the motorway.

'God, I'm wet. Been standing there half an hour. Mind if I take my coat off?' He didn't wait for a reply and threw it on the back seat, a shower of droplets splashing the back of my neck. I was invisible as he rolled up the sleeves of his sweater, brushed his trousers and removed his boots. Steam rose from his socks as he stretched out his feet in the warmth from the heater.

Could he hear how fast my heart was beating? Could he feel the swathe of fear surrounding me? I gripped the steering wheel to stem the imminent shaking. If only I could turn back.

I said nothing as he sorted himself out. Just the wipers swishing and squeaking, fighting the cascade that poured down the windscreen. He wriggled around, adjusted the seat position to recline it and move it further back. His glance said, 'Hope you don't mind?' although he didn't ask. Then he picked up his canvas bag and rummaged in it. He wasn't looking for a weapon, was he? Don't be stupid, I told myself. Surely he wouldn't take his shoes off if he was about to attack.

Out of the corner of my eye I saw him extract a pencil case. The sort children use, oblong with a long zip. He undid it and took out a penknife.

I gasped. I didn't mean to but the sound escaped. He made a noise, a cross between a laugh and a sneer.

'Do you think I'm going to attack you?' He mocked innocently. 'Just going to sharpen a pencil.' And he did.

'Most people use a pencil sharpener,' I muttered.

'Not me. I like the shape a knife creates. Anyway, couldn't do much damage with this knife.' He waved it around, causing me to swerve.

'Bit risky, picking up a stranger. A bloke. And it's getting dark. I'm grateful, of course. Do you often pick up hitch-hikers?'

I was now feeling seriously worried. 'It was Birmingham,' I said. 'I used to live there and I'd stopped before I realised what I was doing. I've never picked up anyone before. I should have driven past.'

'Rubbish. You'll have a story to tell now. Of this guy with a knife.' He laughed at his joke and at me, a single 'Hah'.

Then there was silence. He was making sure I was thinking about it. That's what he was doing. More knife brandishing, a few more pencils sharpened. I tried to glance across, aware of his every move, but not wanting to lose my focus on the river that was the road.

He put his hand back into his bag. 'Do you know what else I've got here?'

I hardly dared to look. He had a small box in his hand.

'Stolen goods. Gold earrings. A birthday present for my girlfriend.'

He waited for my reaction; I could hear him listening.

'I can't afford stuff like this so there's only one way to get it. Don't go in for much theft. Just when necessary. No violence. Just a little sleight of hand.' I sensed the broad grin on his face, the enjoyment my discomfort was giving him. I wondered if he was inspecting the contents of the car, prospecting for his next free gift.

'Want a mint?' He waved a tube at me.

I shook my head.

'It's okay – it wouldn't be receiving stolen goods. I paid for these!'

The smell of peppermint wafted around me. I felt sick and had an intense desire to visit the toilet.

'Nice jacket you're wearing.'

It was. Leather. Cost more than I could afford. Was that his next target? He'd have to get me to stop. My head was a mess of possibilities. Maybe he'd want my handbag; that was expensive. It was on the back seat, next to my overnight bag. Easy game when he reached for his coat. I'd got around £30 in my purse but there were credit cards, too. Where had I put my phone?

'Don't know where I'm staying tonight. Got mates scattered about. Can usually find a sofa somewhere.' He reached across and placed his hand on my arm. I jumped and jarred my neck as I pulled away from him, zig-zagging into the middle lane. The driver behind me sounded his horn, pulled out and mouthed something, his face distorted by the rain. I made out two fingers as he went past.

'Hang on! That was just a friendly pat. Wondered if you have a spare bed? Or a sofa? Even a floor and a blanket?'

'No, No!' I screamed at him. I'd found my voice. 'What a cheek you have! How dare you accept a lift from me, then terrorise me? Pretending violence to frighten me. Boasting about your exploits so I'd feel like a victim. Well, it won't work!'

My anger seemed to please him. He slid down the seat, put his head back and closed his eyes. He started to whistle, a song I half recognised. I turned on the radio to drown him out. It was an orchestral piece, something soothing and quiet. No use.

He took one of his sharpened pencils and a small notebook and started to write.

'Tell me how you feel.'

'Shut up,' I replied.

'I'm serious. Tell me. I suspect you're scared. I know you regret giving me a lift. But you've got me, at least for the next half hour, so we may as well talk.'

What choice did I have?

'Okay.' I hesitated. 'I'm mad at myself for being stupid.'

'Kindness is not stupidity. You stopped to help a sodden young man get to his destination.'

'Not thinking straight is stupid.'

'So think now. What do you think of me?

Anything true might spur him to violence; anything bland might annoy him so much it would have a similar outcome.

'I don't approve of stealing.'

'I don't either.'

'You shouldn't flash a penknife around.'

'You're right. It's not up to the task. My Swiss army knife is better.' He produced it from the bag and slowly opened one of the blades. I could feel tears starting to run down my face. My bladder was bursting.

'This is good. Handy when camping. All sorts of useful gadgets on it. You should get one. Ask Father Christmas.' He proceeded to clean his nails with the blade.

I wiped my hand across my face and sniffed. There were tissues in the glove box but I couldn't ask for them. I'd remembered my phone was in there.

'I don't suppose you smoke?'

'No. And no-one smokes in my car.'

'I have something more interesting than tobacco.'

'I said no.'

'How about sex?'

'What?' This was worse than the knife. My sweaty hands slipped on the steering wheel and I could feel my dress clinging to my damp legs. I hoped I looked as repulsive as I felt.

'Thought that might be an interesting topic to chat about. Just trying to fill the time. Do you enjoy it? Are you still single? Many partners? Always fascinating to compare experiences.' He chuckled to himself. 'Perhaps I should start the ball rolling. I've got through a few. Not in the Russell Brand League but I like variety. Won't go into the details. Would hate to embarrass you! It would embarrass you, wouldn't it? You'll be glad to know I disapprove of rape.'

Then why mention it? Why talk about sex at all?

'I have to stop. I need the toilet.'

'Okay, no problem. Next services.'

Ten minutes later, I'd pulled off the motorway and parked in a well-lit spot, close to the shops. Next to another car. There were people around. I had to make him get out of the car. I wasn't leaving him to rummage, to help himself. Maybe I could be quick, get back to the car before him and leave.

'I could call the police, you know.' Courage came with the proximity of help.

'The police? Why? What are you charging me with? Aggressive sharpening of my pencils? Cleaning my nails with a blade? Don't think there's a law banning cheeky conversations and the odd lie.'

He was right. He undid his seat belt and turned to face me, examining me closely. I shrank into my seat. Then he smiled, a genuine smile, not derisive or sarcastic.

'I'm Jack, by the way.' His voice was softer. He paused. 'I'm not a scrounger or a thief. The earrings aren't stolen. I bought them as a gift and they're not gold, anyway. I don't normally threaten people or lead them to think that's what I'm doing. In fact, I never hitch-hike.

'I'm a crime writer. I'm looking for inspiration, doing some research. My next book is about a psychologically disturbed guy who hitches a lift and then finds himself caught up with crooks. So I need real-life info. I need to know how people react to different situations, real people, proper responses. I take notes in pencil in my note book. I have somewhere to stay tonight – my own home. I'm not sex-mad nor do I use drugs.' He grinned, still enjoying my discomfort.

'Perhaps you don't believe me. That's up to you. It was useful. Thanks.'

He put his boots on, took his coat and left, head bent against the rain. After a few paces, he turned and waved. As I got out of the car to find the loo, a coffee and sanity, I saw him standing by the slip-road with his thumb out, waiting for his next inspiration.

Linda Fawke writes fiction and non-fiction, preferably late at night, and is about to publish her first novel, 'A Taste of his own Medicine'. She was a winner of the Daily Telegraph 'Just Back' travel-writing competition and has published in Mslexia, 'Litro' online, 'Scribble', 'The Oldie' and 'Berkshire Life'.

Website: linimeant.wordpress.com

Tartan Legs

Maureen Cullen

Theresa had another go at the words she'd been practising. Practicing was one thing. Saying them out loud to her mother was quite another. Maybe she should let the gale whisk her off the cliff into the Clyde, roll her down the Firth into the Irish Sea, and from there toss her like a cork, out to the Atlantic.

If only.

She'd just take a wee walk around the scheme to settle her stomach. Why her mother chose to live up here, the most exposed area of the town, high above the Clyde, she couldn't fathom. It was a right trek, so it was. As she turned the corner she set her brolly against the wind like a bin lid but still a lash sopped her nylons.

She almost tumbled over the Crier and the Chronicle. One was the mother of the other but they were identical. The hitch of the brolly, the spindly legs poking out, made them look like crows. Crows that might swoop on her head and peck out her eyes. Aye, like those in the Hitchcock film at The Rialto last week. She rubbed her stomach with the heel of her hand.

'Theresa, hen,' they clacked. Their spokes jabbed her into the neighbour's hedge, cold water seeping in from neck to knickers. One said, 'Off tae see yer ma then?'

'Aye, aye, ah am...'

They leaned in, beady eyes bright. The other said, 'Maggie's lucky tae have a daughter like you. Round every Saturday. Why, jist the other day she said how she didnae know whit she'd dae withoot you. Poor widow wuman that she is.' Theresa's stomach tightened again. 'Ye awright, hen?' she cawed.

'Aye, ah'm fine. Jist dreichet.'

'Oh, ye can say that again. A body could get blown off the cliff ... and jist away tae get a pan loaf.'

A gust of wind rose up and wheeked them round the bend, black raincoats ballooning behind them. Theresa could have sworn they took flight.

The latch of the gate didn't squeak as usual. Funny that, as her Charlie said he was going to oil it after Mass tomorrow. Her mother drew a line at gardening, said that was man's work.

Mum's head floated in the window. Theresa fluttered her fingers. Thank God, it wasn't the weather for the Saturday trip to the cemetery, tramping down there to tend Dad's grave, Mum polishing the lettering, James and Baby son Liam, her auburn head powdered grey, Theresa on the gravel praying.

Praying she'd hurry it up.

Praying for wings so she could stretch away, leave all the soil and supplication behind.

At the doorstep she collapsed the brolly, spewing ice-cold water over her shoes. The front door gave way as she turned the knob, even though Charlie told Mum time and again to keep it locked. 'Maggie, yer a woman on yer ain and there's a lot of drunks and ne'r-dae-wells round here.'

'Ah'm no feart o drunks. Ah'll lock it when the dark comes down and unlock it at first light, as ah've ay done.'

That was the trouble. The fight rose in Theresa's chest and flushed her face. Everything was always the same: skirting boards dusted on Mondays, brasses on a Thursday, floors hoovered daily, coins counted out in columns for the milk boy, the paper boy, the insurance man, the coal man. Her mother ticked her life away to household duty.

Well, Theresa wouldn't be chain-ganged into drudgery.

She stepped into the lobby, soon breathing in a mixture of bleach and polish that set off a bout of sneezes.

Her mother was at the kitchen door. 'Ye're no comin down wi something, hen? Here, gie me that coat. Go on in, sit at the fire.'

Theresa was helpless to stop the tickle in her tubes. Her coat was dragged off, nearly tipping her on her bum. She slipped off her shoes and they fair flew up into her mother's grip, landing at the fire in the living room. Sputtering into her hanky she followed them in.

Mum spun past like a wraith, and in no time the kitchen hatch pinged open. 'Ye'll get yer death of cold in that wee slip of a coat.'

No point telling her that the rain had just been a wee smir when she'd left the flat and it was only up here that the gale blew. Anyway, her mother had already turned to the jigging kettle.

Theresa stood by the grate, shivering despite the spit of flames. Her blouse was pasted to her back. She plucked it out of her skirt, and leaned closer to the fire, scorching her legs just the right side of pain.

Mum came in with the tray. 'Ah made it nice and strong. Och, sit down hen, ye'll get tartan legs.'

When her mother bent to pour the tar, Theresa glanced up at the photo frames either end of the mantelpiece. Lovely Liam... just a wee baby.

Even after all these years she sometimes caught the scent of baby powder when she was in this house.

Liam's photo wasn't there?

In its place was her own wedding photograph. That was usually on the sideboard. She twisted round. No, in its place was some animal ornament or other.

At least Dad was still on the mantel. It would be easier if he was here. She would never have been able to marry Charlie if it hadn't been for Dad.

He'd said it first. 'Theresa has some great news, don't you darlin?'

She'd nodded with one eye on the door.

Mum's eyes darted from him to Theresa.

He said, 'She's winchin Charlie Reid's boy. A nice fella he is too.'

Mum's eyelids batted. 'A... Protestant?'

Her mother hadn't spoken to her for a whole week. Just took on a martyr's slump. Only came round when they got engaged and Charlie promised to marry Theresa in The Chapel.

Theresa twitched as her mother thrust the cup and saucer under her nose, spilling the scalding tea over her hand.

Mum fussed. 'Oh, my God. Ah'm sorry. Ah don't know what's the matter wi me the day.' She rushed out, was soon back with a dripping cloth.

Theresa let her dab and wipe. The hand wasn't sore, but her eyes stung. If only Dad was still here, on his chair by the fire, the flock worn, roll-up tight between his fingers.

On the eve of her wedding, he'd smiled his half-cocked grin, took a drag, rolled the smoke around his mouth, let it coil out. 'Aye, when ah wis a young man, masel, ah hid dreams.'

'Ye can still have dreams, Dad.'

'Aye, aye, but chances don't come round that often. Yer ma didnae like the idea of being a Ten Pound Pom. Naw, she wouldnae leave her ain mother.'

'But Dad, you should have made her go.'

Mum was still dabbing. Theresa concentrated on the lampshade above her mother's head. When the letter had arrived from Australia House three weeks ago, she'd placed it on top of her whites in the dresser drawer.

Mum wittered on. 'Ye awright, hen? Whit a carry on. Yer brother's got a new job. In Glesga. He'll get the train, but. They'll no be movin anyplace. Ah widnae get tae see the weans as much. Mind that's no a bad thing. Ah've got ma ain life tae. Change is guid, dependin...' She placed the teacup back in Theresa's hand before sitting down across from Dad's chair. 'Ah draw a line at pigeon! Imagine eating pigeons. Dirty creatures. Rats wi wings. At the dinner he went tae. Funny stuff folk eat in far off places. Course, I bet there's some lovely fruit ye can get abroad. Theresa are ye listening tae me, hen?'

Just as Theresa was about to open her mouth, her mother was away again. 'Ah nearly forgot tae tell ye. Hannah Gillespie? She's got cancer.' She spelt the word out as if it would blister her lips. 'Life's short so it is. If the fags don't get ye, the weather will. Don't get me wrong, there's a lot tae be said for the outdoor life...'

Theresa tried a sip of the bitter tea. There was something different about her mum today. She looked younger.

'Ah want tae see ma weans get on Theresa hen, ye know that, don't ye?'

'Mum?'

'Aye hen?' She peered into Theresa's face, expectancy in her eyes. Mum thought she was pregnant. That was it. But her mother went on. 'Ah'm sure ye're going under wi something. Ye look awfy... peelly-wally. It's the damp in this place. Ye ay had a bad chest. When ye were wee...'

Theresa's insides see-sawed. Mum counting the shillings for the bills, Mum stewing the tea in the pot, Mum tending the grave.

Theresa said it. 'We're emigrating to Australia. We've been passed and we're off tae Canberra in May.'

Mum's mouth opened and closed in slow motion. Theresa focused on the lips, the filling eyes, the lipstick and violet eye shadow. Lipstick and eye shadow? A lone tear sprang from the corner of one eye and a black thread trailed down one cheek. Mascara? She looked closer. Her mum had Panstick on, she hadn't rubbed it in right, but it was still nice. And rouge. Two dots on her cheeks. And her hair was French-combed into a flurry of bright auburn. Theresa shook away the haze. Mum was half smiling. She was quite pretty when she smiled.

Inching her cup and saucer down, Theresa tuned in.

'Och, hen. Ah wis wondering when ye were gonnae tae tell me. Ah wis under pain of excommunication if ah breathed a word of it tae ye. Father Mills heard it from Jack's mother-in-law's cousin who's off Charlie's pal's family, whitshisname? Remember her, she cleans the chapel house? Father thought ah should know but ah wis tae wait till ye tellt me yersel.'

'What?'

102

Her mother pressed her lips together, moved over to the couch and clamped Theresa's hand under her own. 'Och hen, ye cannae keep a secret in this toon. Don't get me wrong, ah wis heartbroken, ah am. At first ah wis going round tae yer place tae give ye a guid talking tae. Tae tell ye that ye couldnae go. But Father took me aside after the parish jumble sale. He looked me in the eye and he said, "Margaret, you're thinking only of yourself. Your daughter must follow her own path." Yer a clever girl and ye'll never get on here.' She turned, smiled at Dad's photo and whispered, 'He'd never forgive me if ah stopped ye.'

Theresa closed her eyes against the nip of salty tears. Her mother's hand was on her hair, stroking, the other on her cheek, fingers soft as eiderdown. She peeked through heavy lashes.

'Mum, ye've had yer hair done.'

'Aye, de ye like it?' She patted her lacquered head. 'Ah thought it wis time ah bucked masel up.'

'What?' Theresa's breath was stuck back of her throat. The fire had swallowed all the air in the room.

'Ye've got to live yer ain life, hen. Ah've got the grandweans and ah'll get the phone in. It'll be awright. We've come through worse and we're still in one piece.'

The dam Theresa had battened down burst. All the certainty in her life was floating away to be replaced by what? Joeys and sunshine? Joeys? Her head rubber banded to the sideboard. A figure of a kangaroo with her joey peeking out of the sack greeted her. Love from Australia was etched on its hat, a hat with corks hanging in a circle.

Maureen Cullen writes short stories and poetry. She lives in Argyll and Bute with her husband, close to extended family. A retired social worker, she hasn't looked back since a friend suggested taking an Open University course in Creative Writing. Every day she sets pen to paper and surprises herself.

Counting Squirrels

Jacqui Cooper

MONDAY

Cassie hadn't been on a bus in years and wouldn't be on one now if her car hadn't broken down. The bus journey was not a pleasant experience. The windows were steamed from the crush of people and the rather large man who had squeezed into the seat beside her was sitting on her good woollen coat. In the aisle, school children scrapped and shouted. Behind her, two women discussed a programme they had watched on TV last night, marvelling at the skill of the detective and the intricacies of the plot. Cassie, too, had watched the programme. She itched to turn round and tell them that the story just wasn't that complicated, but of course she did no such thing.

The bus idled at the lights beside the park gates. Glancing out of the window, Cassie noticed a squirrel poised on a wall. Whiskers twitching, the little creature stared back at her until the bus moved off.

By the time Cassie reached the office, she was fuming at the time she had lost on the journey. As her staff began to trickle in, many of them eagerly dissecting last night's detective show, she pointedly closed her office door on their chatter and got to work.

TUESDAY

Her car was still off the road but the route the bus had taken yesterday had given Cassie an idea. By road she had to navigate the town's one way system but if she walked to work through the park, she reasoned she could get there in a fraction of the time.

When she'd bought her house the estate agent had been quick to point out the proximity of the park but Cassie was not a friend of nature. In the four years she had lived here, she had never once been in it. This early in the morning, though, it revealed itself to be a surprisingly pleasant, leafy haven.

It quickly became clear that her expensive, stylish shoes were not made for walking. Holding on to the arm of a bench, she levered one shoe off to rub her heel. And saw a squirrel on the bench not two feet away, head cocked, watching her. Cassie gave a shriek and brandished her shoe. The squirrel shot off.

'You frightened him.'

A man in a high visibility jacket stood on the grass verge holding some kind of gardening implement. Wobbling precariously on one foot, Cassie crammed her shoe back on.

'Not half as much as he frightened me,' she said. 'I prefer my wildlife viewed through a TV screen.'

He laughed, though she hadn't intended her comment as a joke.

'Then let's hope he doesn't chase you. You'd have a hard time getting away in those shoes.'

Chase her? Her eyes widened in alarm until she realised he was joking. Cassie pursed her lips. She was far too busy for jokes or idle chatter. With a polite goodbye and her head in the air, she stalked off.

WEDNESDAY

The next day she chose more sensible shoes and found herself slowing when she neared the park bench where she'd seen the squirrel. Sure enough she saw the little creature balanced at an impossible angle on a tree trunk, nose quivering, one tiny paw outstretched towards her. Was he begging? If so, he was out of luck.

What did squirrels eat anyway? Ah. Nuts, of course. She peered into the branches of his tree though she had no idea why – she would only know a nut tree if it grew little bags of salted peanuts.

'He likes you, that one. He doesn't talk to just anyone.'

It was the man again. Cassie saw a council truck parked a short way away so presumably he was a gardener. 'You can tell them apart?' she asked, sceptically.

'Of course. That little guy? He's a scamp. In fact that's what I call him.'

'Right.' There didn't seem much more to say. 'Well I'd better-' Another squirrel joined the first and a noisy squabble broke out between them.

The gardener gave a satisfied sigh. 'Good. A two squirrel day.'

Cassie had a pile of work waiting at the office. She should be on her way. But she couldn't let that go. 'A two squirrel day?'

He nodded. 'A two squirrel day means I get a bacon butty for lunch. The council wrote it into my contract.'

That didn't sound likely and she frowned. 'They did?'

'No,' His blue eyes twinkled and she realised he was teasing her again.

People didn't tease Cassie. They just didn't. She really should go. But she didn't move. 'If a two squirrel day means a bacon sandwich, what happens on a three squirrel day?' she asked.

His smile widened. 'A three squirrel day is the best kind of day. Last three squirrel day I found a tenner when I was sweeping up leaves. I'm Jack by the way.'

Cassie had no intention of introducing herself to a strange man in a park, even if he was a council employee. But nothing good awaited her at the office today so despite her better judgement, she lingered. 'What about a four squirrel day? Or a five?'

He scratched his chin. 'A four day can be good or bad. Best I can say about a four squirrel day is it's unpredictable. But a five...' He sucked in a breath. 'Five or above means chaos. No order to the day. A five squirrel day, given the chance, I'd stay home in bed.'

This was ridiculous. Cassie could not believe they were having this conversation, but still, her lips twitched. 'What about a no squirrel day?'

Something shifted in his expression and his smile faded. 'I've done my share of no squirrel days. I've no inclination to do another.'

The peculiar conversation still ran through Cassie's head as she neared the office. Passing a café she had to fight the impulse to buy a bacon sandwich. Instead she bought a box of doughnuts to share with the team, who looked pleased but surprised as she put the offering in the tiny kitchen. Was the boss buying doughnuts really so unusual?

Lips pursed, she shut her office door.

THURSDAY

Cassie was running late. Luckily her shoes were even more sensible today, making it easier to hurry.

Although she watched out for him, she didn't see Jack. She did see three squirrels running over the grass and tried to remember. Three was good, wasn't it? And then she saw the fourth and frowned. What had he said? Four was unpredictable.

She shook her head at the stupidity of forecasting her day with squirrels. But she had already been dreading work today, so the four squirrels tipped the balance. Cassie knew everyone thought she revelled in being the boss of her event planning company, but actually, she was under immense pressure. Ten people relied on her to pay their wages and put food on the table. Which meant that if an employee didn't pull their weight, she had to let them go for the sake of the others.

Cassie had a very uncomfortable conversation ahead of her today. But still, thinking about the squirrels, she held off calling Todd, the newest member of the team into the office. Just as well because he burst in anyway in a flurry of excitement.

'Ms Turner, you will never believe what happened! I was out with my mates last night and I overheard this couple arguing. They were due to get married next year but she's got a job abroad so they're bringing the wedding forward and he wants to make it a small affair, but she says, no we should still go all out-'

'Todd-'

'So he says how are we going to arrange that at short notice-'

'Todd-'

'And she started crying because she wanted her new job but she also wanted her big day-'

'TODD!'

He stopped for breath and grinned. 'I butted in and said I could help. I mean we could, the firm, I mean. And they said give them a price. They need marquees, caterers, cars the lot. We can do that, can't we?'

Cassie nodded. 'Yes, of course we can. We'll need to gather everyone for a meeting. Organise that, will you? And Todd? Well done.'

He left, looking pleased. Thank goodness she hadn't fired him. He was right for the company. Or he would be once she had moved him to a new position in sales.

She shook her head ruefully: a four squirrel day. Unpredictable, just as Jack had said.

FRIDAY

The sun shone on Friday morning. Cassie took her time walking to work even though she had yet another busy day ahead. She saw Jack's truck parked by the lake.

'Enjoying the view?' she asked.

He smiled. 'Each new season brings its own pleasures.'

'I don't really notice the seasons when I'm driving,' she admitted.

'Are you having car trouble? Is that why you are walking?'

Actually her car was parked outside her house and had been since Wednesday. Should she confess she was enjoying the fresh air? That the walk cleared her head? That her skirt felt looser and she was sleeping better? She didn't say any of that. Instead she looked around. 'Where's Scamp?'

Jack nodded to where two squirrels chased each other over the grass. He didn't look at Cassie but cleared his throat. 'Two squirrels. I'll have my bacon butty by the lake today. About 12.30.'

A date? Cassie had no idea but she felt flushed and distracted for the rest of the morning.

At 12.15 she grabbed her bag. 'I'm going to lunch.' A stunned silence met her words. She might as well have said she was going out to buy an ostrich.

She was in such a hurry to get to the park, she forgot to buy a sandwich.

Jack was already on the bench. When she dropped down beside him he handed her a wrapped bacon sandwich, crispy bacon on crusty bread.

Cassie realised she was starving. 'I usually work through lunch,' she admitted.

'Everyone is in such a hurry these days.'

'Well there's so much to do, isn't there?' she said, thinking about the emails to be answered, the work she would have to take home at the weekend-

'See those ducks?' Jack broke into her thoughts.

She glanced at the lake.

'Are they rushing?' he asked.

Cassie laughed. The ducks were gliding, the very picture of tranquillity. 'No.'

Jack nodded. 'Yet they do everything we do. The essential stuff any way. They find food. They find a mate. They build a home, raise a family, keep them warm and fed and safe. Yet have you ever seen a duck looking stressed?'

She laughed. 'Now you mention it, no.'

'We could all learn a thing or two from nature,' Jack said. 'We need to take a step back and reduce our stress levels or nature will find a way to make us pay more attention.'

Something about his tone made her ask, 'I take it you haven't always been a gardener?'

'Not always,' he admitted. 'I used to work in finance. Now I take lessons from ducks.'

'And you count squirrels.'

'It's better than counting blood pressure.'

She absorbed the message in that. 'I'm thinking of joining the park run at the weekend.'

'And you're having lunch today,' he approved. 'You've already slowed down. You have more colour in your cheeks, too.'

'I'm getting a life,' she agreed. 'What about you?'

He looked at her with twinkling blue eyes and smiled. 'Do you know, I think I might be getting a life too.'

Jacqui Cooper writes short stories and has been published in various women's magazines. She loves entering competitions and even occasionally win some.

Jacqui lives in Yorkshire and spends too much time dreaming of traveling to far flung places. Unlike most writers she doesn't have a novel currently on the go and much prefers short stories.

Twitter: @jacqcooper

In the Pink

Tracy Davidson

My landlady knocks on the door and lets herself in. I wonder why she bothers knocking at all if she's not going to wait to be invited. I must get a bolt for the door. It's really rude of her, but she's such a friendly lady I don't like to complain.

She waves a piece of post at me, smiling broadly.

"Look Ellie," she says. "You've got an admirer!" She hands the pink envelope over to me.

I had forgotten it was Valentine's Day. Not that I was expecting anything. My young man is away in the war somewhere. I say 'my young man', but he isn't really. We only met the once, at a dance, the week before he was called up. He had the loveliest smile I'd ever seen. A good dancer too. He kissed me on the cheek and promised to write, when he could.

I've not heard anything since. I hope he's all right.

The landlady hovers by the door, waiting for me to open the card. I mentally add 'nosey' to 'likes to barge in' on my list of irritations with her. I smile and thank her politely, glancing towards the door. Thankfully she takes the hint and leaves, looking a little disappointed.

I wait for a moment, just in case she decides to pop back in, pretending to have forgotten something. She doesn't.

I hold the envelope up in front of me. I don't recognise the writing, not that I know what Peter's writing looks like. There are no foreign marks, it was posted locally. Though I guess someone could have posted it for him.

I open the envelope carefully. I hate to tear things, and the pink is such a lovely shade. The card inside is just as pretty, the cover full of blooms. There's a lovely verse – sweet, but not too sickly for a man to send. I read the handwritten comments: "To the beautiful girl who danced with me. With love always. P."

At the bottom is a postscript: "I'll be visiting you this morning. I can't wait!" Oh my! It is from Peter. And he's coming here. I hope he's not been injured. But how does he know I live here? I can't remember exactly when I moved out from my parents house. A while ago anyway.

No matter. He's coming. He thinks I'm beautiful, and he loves me! No-one's ever said that to me before. Boys never showed much interest growing up. A combination of natural shyness, a nervous stutter, and a scar on my cheek from a childhood accident, meant a distinct lack of suitors. Peter was the first, and only, one to see beyond these things. That evening we spent together – talking, dancing and holding hands – was the best night of my life. I went to bed with such a huge smile on my face.

I can't wait to see him again either. I just hope I'm not a disappointment. Hope he still sees the real me inside, that he doesn't take one look and wonder what he ever saw in me.

I must make a little effort. Unlike my girlfriends, I'm not keen on make-up. The way I do it always seems to draw attention to my faults, instead of disguise them. Perhaps my landlady will help. As much as I didn't want her to interfere earlier, now I wish she would.

I suspect she's a bit psychic, because just as I'm deciding to go and find her, along comes another knock at the door. She pops her head round, looks surprised when I beckon her in.

"It's just me – Mrs Wilson," she says. "I came to remind you about breakfast. Most of the others have finished theirs. You'll have to be quick if you want something cooked."

I'm far too excited to eat. I shake my head impatiently and wave the card at her, much like she waved it at me earlier.

"My young man is back from the war Mrs Wilson," I say. "He...Peter...is coming this morning to see me."

Mrs Wilson smiles. "That's lovely Ellie dear," she says. "Do you need any help getting dressed?"

I look down at myself and realise I'm still in my nightdress. I hadn't even noticed. I check the time – nearly 9.00. I must have overslept. I head straight for the wardrobe. I know exactly what I want to wear.

"Yes, please, Mrs Wilson," I say. "I've no idea what time Peter's coming and I want to look nice for him. Could you help me find my pink dress with the white collar. I can't seem to see it here. And then help me with make-up."

"Of course I'll help dear," she says. "But I don't remember a dress like that. Are you sure you brought it with you?"

"Oh yes, it's my favourite," I say. "Mother bought it for my 16th birthday. I was wearing it the night Peter and I met. He said I looked perfect in it."

"Oh," says Mrs Wilson, frowning. She looks at me for a moment, her head on one side. She looks like she's trying to figure out a way to tell me something.

"It's not damaged is it?" I ask anxiously. "Or been stolen?"

115

"No, no dear, nothing like that," Mrs Wilson assures me. "It's just...it's being laundered, that's all. Yes, I remember now. I'm afraid it won't be ready in time."

Disappointed, I turn back to look at the contents of the wardrobe. Nothing looks right, or even familiar. It all looks terribly dowdy to me, like things my mother, or even my grandmother, would wear. I wonder how many of my good things are in the laundry.

The only thing that catches my eye is a knitted pink cardigan on the top shelf. It's exactly the same shade as my missing dress. It will have to do. Peter could arrive at any minute.

With Mrs Wilson's help I don a plain dress and put the pink cardi on top. Then she does my make-up for me. She has a light touch and looks pleased when she's finished.

Before I can check my reflection in the mirror, there's a knock at the door.

"Oh Mrs Wilson, do you think that's him?"

"Only one way to find out," she says, going to open it.

I take a deep breath and wait for the handsome boy I remember to walk in. The man who enters carries a bouquet of pink flowers in front of him. But it's not Peter. This man is old and grey. He has a pleasant face, lined with old scars. I feel a pang of sympathy for him, and wish now I hadn't made Mrs Wilson cover up my own.

"Can I help you?" I ask. "I think you have the wrong room."

He smiles at this, a little sadly I think, and glances at Mrs Wilson.

"We're a little confused today," she says.

116

I frown. What does she mean by "we're"? She leaves the room before I can query it, shutting me in with this strange man. I look at his face again. He has Peter's eyes. A relative perhaps. Clearly, I'm supposed to know him.

He goes straight to the mantelpiece and puts the flowers in an empty vase. He comes and sits in the chair opposite mine and puts a box of chocolates on the table. My stomach rumbles, reminding me I missed breakfast.

"How are you feeling today Ellie love?" he asks.

"Um... fine, thanks," I say. "And... and you?"

He leans forward, smiling, and pats my hand. "All the better for seeing you," he says.

The feel of his hand on mine seems strangely familiar, and comforting. I find myself gripping it and hanging on.

"Look at the photos love," he says, nodding towards the sideboard. I look at the line-up of photos I hadn't even noticed this morning, until now.

The first one is of Peter and me, on the night of our dance. The only photo I have of him. Or so I thought. But the next photo is of us too, wearing different clothes. The third photo of us has me in a wedding dress, Peter in full uniform. I scan the rest of the photos. Peter and me holding a baby, his handsome face marred by fresh scars. I squeeze the hand I'm holding a little tighter. The black and white photos are followed by colour ones – Peter and me with two children, then three. Then an older version of us, smiling proudly either side of a young man at graduation. Finally, a photo of us holding another baby, but we're old and grey now.

The cloud lifts a little and I remember... some things anyway. Most is a blur. But one thing I do know – this man is my Peter, my husband, who came back from the war scarred but in one piece. And we've had a good life together.

I look at him again. "I love you," I say.

"Ditto," he replies.

I don't ever want to forget again....

...I wake up in a chair. It's broad daylight. I must have dozed off. An elderly man with kind eyes stoops toward me, kisses me gently on the cheek.

"I have to go now Ellie," he says. "I'll come and see you again soon."

I smile and nod politely, though I have no idea who he is, or why there are tears on his cheeks as he waves at me from the door. I shall have to warn mother not to let strange men in the house again. This is wartime after all.

Tracy Davidson from Warwickshire writes poetry and flash fiction. Her work has appeared in various publications and anthologies, including: Poet's Market 2015, Mslexia, The Binnacle, Modern Haiku, A Hundred Gourds, Atlas Poetica, Journey to Crone, Ekphrastia Gone Wild, The Great Gatsby Anthology and In Protest: 150 Poems for Human Rights.

Twitter: @tracydavidson27

The Coffee Business

Clare Girvan

So she says, 'I've had a lovely evening.'

She's got her key in the door and turning back as if she's just thought of something and I know what she's going to say - 'Would you like to come in for coffee?' in a casual sort of voice, as if it's only just occurred to her, like only good manners. Would you like a coffee after sitting through a reshowing of The Phantom of the Opera at the Picture House, which I only suggested because it was the kind of thing my mate Kelvin said you should take girls to.

'Show them your feminine side,' he said. 'Can't go wrong with a big picture and lots of music and passion. Gives them ideas.'

She's right, it's been a great evening; we've got on like a house on fire, laughing and chatting all the way back to her flat, and I really want to see her again. But I'm going to have to say no. Not because I don't want to go in - I do - but because I shan't know what she means. 'Would you like to come in for a coffee?' - is that a genuine offer, Come in for a coffee and we'll have a chat and then you go home, or will it be code for something else? And if it is, what exactly is it a code for?

Kelvin says 'Sex, obviously, you muppet. It saves embarrassment. It only means one thing when they invite you in for coffee.'

But it's not just that. If I go in, she's going to put the light on, and maybe she won't have noticed the full extent of the Thing until then and she won't know what to do. Kelvin's used to my face. He doesn't really notice it these days. He used to take the mick a bit at school, but then he settled down and we became good mates. But it comes as a shock to other people and I get stared at a lot. I'm kind of used to it and most days I'm not too

bothered, but other days I get really pissed off with getting that kind of attention.

It's not that I haven't been with girls before, I have, I'm not a virgin or anything like that, but it's usually only a certain type of girl. Easy girls, easy in the sense that they don't put you through hoops. A few drinks, 'It's OK, my flatmate's out,' and up the stairs and onto the bed, or even in the back of the car. And you don't have to stay till morning and face them sober in the cold light of day. It's not the best way of doing things but it's easy. Easier. But that's not what I really want. I want a girl for more than that.

I meet a lot of them at clubs. I like clubs. People don't notice so much. The lighting's not too good, darkness and flashing, so by the time you've decided which one you fancy, she's usually too bladdered to notice you've got a huge red birthmark across half your face.

Sometimes one will say, 'You got something wrong with your face?' so I say, 'What's up, haven't you ever seen anyone from the planet Zag before?' and she'll laugh and look a bit embarrassed, so I'll say something like, 'Do you fancy an out of this world experience, then?' and she'll say, 'OK, why not?' Weird, that. And they always want to touch it, too, see what it feels like. I used to wonder if I'd be the same if it was a girl who'd got what I've got, although it's different for girls. They can use make-up.

There's some that I've been out with for a few weeks, but when they say yes, you never know if it's because they want to seem cool about being seen with someone like me or if they feel sorry for you, and when it finishes, you never know for sure whether it was the Thing and getting stared at all the time or something else.

'Oh, it's not you,' they say. 'I'm not ready.'

I never ask, just in case. Kelvin says, 'Don't worry about it, mate. Play the field.' Not that his girls last all that long either.

Or the worst thing, when someone starts coming on to you and they're - well, it's a bit off for me to say it, considering - but a bit minging, you know, the ones no one takes much interest in because they're fat or got nasty teeth or something. And you know they're thinking they're onto a sure thing with you, because you'll be so grateful. One of them even said to me once, 'Oh, come on, it's not as if you've got all that much choice, is it?' So I said, 'Look who's talking,' which I was sorry about afterwards, because it's not a nice thing to say to a girl, even though she deserved it.

But now and then one like this Gina turns up, definitely not the sort you'd bonk in the back of a Nissan, and you're not sure what you're supposed to do or why she's agreed to go

out with you, and you're scared to make a move in case it's the wrong one, and it gets to the coffee business, and you're stuffed. So I go and say, 'No, thanks,' and they look awkward for having asked and say, 'Goodnight, then,' and close the door and that's it.

I met Gina in bright daylight, coming out of the library. My computer was acting up and I was going in to use theirs just as she was coming out and she bumped into me and dropped her book. I couldn't believe her. She was gorgeous, older than me, about twenty two, heavy dark hair tucked behind one ear and falling in a curved point round the other side of her face, big brown eyes, mouth a little bit lopsided, cute.

'Here, let me help,' I said. 'Can I carry it to your car?'

She laughed, tweaking her hair forward. She had a catchy sort of giggly laugh, but not silly.

'It's only one book,' she said. She didn't seem to notice the Thing.

The least I can do,' I said, so we walked to her car, chatting really easily, and I askedher out.

It's funny, I wouldn't normally have asked someone like her, especially not when she'd seen the Thing. They usually come up with some reason - I'm going on holiday, or I have to study, or I've got to visit my gran - anything, and I'd have to smile and pretend it was OK. But we were getting on so well, it just seemed like the natural thing to do - 'Do you fancy going to see a film or something?'

We had a bit of an argument about which one - 'No, we'll see one that you like,' sort of thing - until we decided on The Phantom of the Opera, which isn't really my thing at all, but she hadn't seen it and somehow, seeing it with her, it kind of got to me, all the music and stuff, just like Kelvin said, except that it was supposed to be her it was getting to.

So here we are after a great evening, the coffee business looming, and I'm wondering what to do. Suppose I said, 'That would be nice,' and went in, what if she started giving me choices, like 'Would you prefer tea? Or perhaps something a bit stronger?' and I wouldn't mind a beer, actually, but she probably wouldn't have that in, only a bottle of wine or something. Would she have Coke in? Coke would be good.

Kelvin always says, 'Coffee will be fine,' with a smile, because he knows he's not going to get round to drinking it. Then he sits on the sofa while she's in the kitchen and makes himself at home, picks up a mag or whatever, so he's got something to talk about when she comes back in; probably something girly like shoes or celebrity goss, but he says it shows an interest, shows you're the kind of bloke that can talk about women's things, because they just love that and you're halfway in. But ought you to sit on the sofa, treating her like a servant or your mum or something, or should you go and lean casually in the doorway, as if you're ready to help if she wants you to?

This is what's been whizzing through my mind, but I really like her and I've only got the one chance. And she's turning, and I'm just bracing myself for what's coming, when she says, 'There's something I ought to tell you.'

Oh, shit. She's married. Living with someone. Bound to be, being that gorgeous.

'Go on, then,' I say.

She doesn't say anything, just turns towards the street light and lifts her hair back. I can't believe it. I've spent all evening with her, driven her home, and never noticed. A great long scar from the end of her eyebrow across her cheek to her chin, puckering the skin, pulling her mouth a bit sideways. But if you're not looking for something, you don't see it, do you, and she's had her hair over it and been sitting on my other side all the time. No wonder she wasn't bothered about the Thing. I stare at it. It's horrible, even in lamplight.

'A car crash,' she says. 'Three years ago.'

'Can I touch it?'

She nods. It feels smooth, but lumpy underneath.

'Can you feel that?' I ask.

'Not much. It's really ugly. Do you mind?'

And suddenly, I don't.. 'No. I can't talk, anyway. Does it put blokes off ?' Which is a bit of a cheek to ask, but she kind of shrugs and says, 'Sometimes. Some don't mind and some do.'

And I'm thinking, Jeez, what if we started going out together, both looking like we do with our funny faces. People would really be staring then. And you know what, I don't care. Maybe I would have been put off at first if I'd known about it, but I wouldn't care, I just wouldn't, I'd feel really proud of her, and -

Then she smiles and puts her hand up to the Thing and strokes it, not like they usually do, like they're expecting it to feel like lizard or something, but gently, used to touching freaky skin. Her face is very close, and this might be the right time to kiss her, and she might be expecting it, but I'm not going to. Not yet.

And she's touching mine and I'm touching hers, and I don't care what that sounds like, because it's bloody great actually, and all at once I know exactly what to do.

She's just starting to say, 'Would you like - ' at the same time as I'm starting to say, 'Would you like - ' and we laugh and she says, 'You first.'

If I was a gentleman I'd let her go first, but she still might come up with the coffee business, so I say, 'Would you like to go for a coffee tomorrow?' and she laughs and says,

'That's just what I was going to say. That would be lovely.'

And she leans forward and gives me a little soft kiss on my red, scaly cheek.

Clare Girvan is an ex-biker who escaped from teaching to live in a pretty Devon estuary town and devote herself to writing. She has won prizes and commendations in many short story competitions, but now concentrates chiefly on writing plays, which have been performed in various locations around the country.

www.claregirvan.co.uk

With Deepest Regret

Kelly Turner

I've just finished my shift and I'm certainly glad of it. My feet are throbbing and swollen from all the walking, and now my shoes are pinching. Not that I'm complaining though, this job means a lot to me. While my Fred is off fighting it brings me in a wage as well as keeping me busy, and that can't be a bad thing. And the marvel of being able to call myself a postwoman. Just two years ago that would have been impossible. It was all Fred's idea really, if you cut that man in half he would have "Postie" written through him like a stick of Brighton rock. He's worked for the Post Office since he was a lad, starting off as a messenger boy and moving up through the ranks, so it made sense to him that when war broke out he would join the Post Office Rifles. And he joined up pretty quick too. He was keen to do his bit, right from the start. We were still courting at the time, but we got married soon after. Fred said that he wanted me to make an honest man out of him before he shipped out and thought I ought to get a job. "They'll still need people to deliver the mail," he had said. And for the most part I love it, although as the fighting has gone on its got harder.

I know that people have mixed feelings when they see me marching up their street in my blue coat, skirt and hat, because I've been in their shoes. Is she delivering good news or bad? There have been times after a big push that silence marks my path. I see curtains twitching and I can almost hear the prayers of those inside. "Please God let her walk on by our house. Let him be safe. Let him be alive." Being the bearer of bad news is difficult for me too. Yesterday I delivered another letter to another young woman, probably not long married, just like me. I watched her hand shake as she reached for the envelope. Her voice was barely a whisper as she said "I can't read."

I've been through this before and because it happens so often the Post Office has its rules about it. I asked if she had a neighbour who could read it for her, but she shook her head and asked if I could read it for her.

"Of course I will," I said, and followed her into the house removing my hat as I did so. She offered me a seat, but I said that I was happy to stand. She sat in her armchair, back straight and hands clasped on her lap as I opened the envelope and started to read. "It is my painful duty to inform you that your husband Private Jack Peterson was killed in action this evening. He died bravely and instantaneously." I continued to read, glancing up at her occasionally, but her face was like a mask. "I'm so sorry for your loss, " I said when I had finished, but she didn't seem to hear me, she continued to stare off into the distance. I wondered what it was she saw. Was she looking back at the past, her wedding day maybe, or was she imagining the man she loved cut down in a field of mud and death. I laid the letter onto the table and left her to her grief.

Do you know how many letters the Post Office deals with every day? The war has added millions of letters and parcels to the work that the Post Office was doing already. There are many women writing to soldiers that they have never met. My friend Ethel took up the call to write to a lonely soldier at the front, and now she's engaged to him. Although the Post Office does its best, with this amount of work occasionally mistakes are made. One of the girls I work with told me the story of a friend of hers. She was writing to her husband as we all do, telling him all the little things that were happening at home and sending him parcels. He would write back, thanking her for the home comforts she sent and reassuring her that he was doing ok. Then his letters stopped. She started to worry, obviously, but hadn't got a letter from her husband's commanding officer, so tried to stay positive and carried on writing to him. One day a parcel arrived for her. Inside were her husband's bible, name tags and belongings alongside the unopened letters she had been writing to him.

She knew straight away what had happened, but it was another two days before she got the letter telling her he had died.

And then there was this morning. I delivered a letter to Mrs Collins down the road from me. She took one look at the writing on the front of the envelope and collapsed in tears on the doorstep. I knelt beside her, and put my hand on her shoulder. "It's from Stan" she said. Her Stan had died a couple of weeks ago. I helped her to her feet, and back inside away from the prying eyes of the neighbours. I know I was on duty, but what else could I have done? I put the kettle onto boil, and made us a pot of tea while she read the letter. When I came back in her tears had stopped, although she was dabbing under her eyes with her handkerchief.

"He said he had been shot in the leg, but that it wasn't too bad." She made a little choking sound, somewhere between a sob and a laugh. "Silly sod, he did always try to see the best in every situation."

I took a sip of my tea. "Did you get a letter from his CO?"

"Yes. He said the wound became infected, and they had to amputate. He lost a lot of blood, and didn't come round after the operation." She started to cry again.

"What else does Stan say in his letter?"

"He says he thinks about me every day and he can't wait to see me again." She looked up at me and hugged her arms to her body. "What am I going to do without him?"

I didn't know what to say, so said nothing. We sat in silence for a bit, my hand resting on hers, before I had to take my leave.

The news affects everyone in different ways though, and some reactions you never forget. Just after I started the job I delivered a letter to a woman whose friend was visiting. They both stood on the doorstep as I handed the envelope over. I was never sure what to do back then, and tended to wait around until someone gave me leave to go. The woman ripped open the envelope, and exhaled loudly. "He's dead," She said. She started to cry, and clasped the crucifix at her neck. "Oh thank God, he's dead." I stared at them in disbelief.

Her friend placed an arm around her shoulder. "He'll not lay a hand on you or the children again. Not where he's gone."

"I was so worried about what would happen when the war was over." She placed a shaking hand onto her chest.

"Well now you don't have to. You can move on."

The woman looked up at me and smiled. I'll never forget that smile. "Thank you so much," she said.

I stop off on the way home to visit Mrs Taylor. She is in her sixties, and has been a widow for many years She has three sons away fighting. One is in Italy, and the other two are in France. She is so proud of them. Fred and I have not been blessed with children yet, but I can't imagine what it must be like to send them off to war. Me and Mrs Taylor meet up a lot and talk over tea and cake.

"I got a letter from George today," she tells me. "His friend Burt died when they were on patrol together. German sniper got him."

"Poor George. That must have affected him deeply."

"I think it has. You know what George is like though, he is always trying to spare me from the details, and puts a brave face on." She smooths

128

the napkin on her lap. "He mentions Burt in one sentence, and then goes straight onto a description of the weather."

I smile, "Fred is like that too. It's as if he thinks he's protecting me, but my mind just fills in the gaps."

I know a lot about the situation at the front, mainly from Mrs Taylor and her son Albert, who unlike his brother spares no details. If it makes it through the censor then it makes it into the letter. It's from Albert that we know about the mud, the rats, the fleas. We learn about night watch in the rain, the best way to sit so that the rain pours off your helmet and avoids travelling down into the back of your coat. And we hear about the guns, the relentless noise that shakes you to your core. But from everyone, including Fred and George we learn about the camaraderie. I am so grateful to the boys who fight alongside Fred. They are the family that look after him until he can come back to me.

The afternoon is drawing in, the dull October light is fading, and so I give my thanks to Mrs Taylor and make for home. There's a chill in the air as I step outside, and I draw my coat tighter around me. Goosebumps prickle my arms, and I rub them to keep warm. I walk round the corner back to my home, and see one of my colleagues standing on my doorstep. She looks like she has been there for some time, she has her back to me. I watch her shift her weight from side to side to keep away the cold. Then she turns around and sees me. She is in uniform, and holds a buff coloured envelope in her hands. My legs suddenly feel weak as I step towards her. She moves towards me her arm extended. "I'm so sorry," she says. I look at the envelope, see the stamp of the field hospital and I know. Before I even open the letter, I know.

Since starting to write seriously three years ago, **Kelly Turner** has tried her hand at different styles. She enjoys writing various genres, from history to fantasy with a bit of contemporary fiction in between. She is currently working on my first novel length piece which is set in the modern day.

Twitter: @kellyvturner81

Seeing in the Dark

Laura Morgan

She catches scraps of radio chat, the chorus of songs, registers motorway signs but not the distances, because the biggest part of her is thinking about him. There is a depth to these silences that reminds her of being underwater. She tries to surface, but to do so requires effort, and instead all she can manage is to watch the speedometer while his face bobs in her mind.

Once she's through Inverness she adjusts the angle of her foot on the pedal. Now the silence laps about as she starts to take in more of her surroundings. Darkness swaddles the moor around Crask where the RSPB has yet to fell the old spruce plantation. The wind has torn up the trees to the north and their slanting trunks are weathered the same grey as the sky. She sees how these pale strands matt the green swathe as the dead are held up by the living, and wonders at how their bearing down doesn't rip new roots from the earth.

She checks her rear-view as she brakes coming down Braetongue, forgetting, as she has these whole eleven hours, that her duvet is jammed into the back window. No matter. Now Sarah is on the home straight, the same road she travelled every day on the bus from the high school. She drives the last seven miles with one hand on the wheel.

When she thinks of this place, a bare strip of coast with nothing beyond but the blue shadow of Orkney, she always pictures it as it is in winter. Moorland grass, pale as sand, mounds of rusted bracken, and that dark ruin pointing into the mist, down where the land runs out. But now, in summer, whin bursts from the ditches, tattered bog cotton flows down to the sea – the owld ruin just a scar on the headland. She is thinking of Malcolm again. Part of her can imagine him sitting next to her in the car – how his knees would fall open, how his face would look as he turned from the window. But he was never a passenger in her car. Crazy to think they were that young. And with something between torture and awe, she counts back the years.

They used to go up by the crag late at night. Sit there, looking out to sea. Smoke one of Malcolm's mam's cigarettes or share a bottle of Sweetheart stout left over from the New Year. Far below, there was always a creel boat listing on the dusky sand, floats strung up on the gunwale, seaweed dripping from the painter. Malcolm would talk about the horsepower, the pot-hauler on its stern. She'd point to a tanker on the horizon, snatch the fag from his mouth.

At the turn off for the village, she flicks the indicator. Clutch in, she sits a moment in the empty road before slipping the Corsa into first. It's the same every year. She will settle after a few days. Pick some brambles, walk the dog. But when she first comes back, all she sees are memories. That house – long someone's holiday home with a neat grass lawn and a climbing rose – that was the old primary school. Malcolm invented the game one windy day, the day they were late for the bell. There were no rules exactly. Just leaning into the gusts, the currents juddering between your jumper and coat, and great muffled claps at your ears.

The sun shines in puddles in the yard. Sarah parks by the tumbledown barn and gets out to the smell of emptiness. At the other side of the fence is an owld bath the yowes drink from. The taps still on it, gleaming in the sun. Her mam appears from the byre behind a flurry of hens.

'Come here to me,' she says.

Sarah leaves the rucksack she was pulling from the boot and gives her mam a hug. It was only this time last year that Sarah saw her, but her skin looks older – another year of screwing up her eyes in that harsh coastal light. They leave Sarah's bag in the hall and go to put the kettle on. Her mam gives her all the big news in the village. Only half-listening,

Sarah looks around at the ship's bell on the dresser, the chipped skirting boards, the wire cutters next to the toaster. And more then ever she has the feeling of Malcolm being there, that these were spaces he once filled. It's not his ghost. It's too real for that.

Somehow the game had continued. Years later, up on the crag at night, the two of them had taken it in turns to stand near the edge. It had to be a northerly and it had to be gale. Leaning into the gloom, you felt the sea's ghost pass through you. But even in a big storm there'd be a moment when the wind snapped itself taut – the clapping in your ears gone, the sea suddenly loud – and you felt yourself balancing on your toes and realised that you hadn't been leaning all that far.

That last conversation on Sarah's doorstep. She liked to taunt herself with it, playing it over in her head. She'd just got back from her first term at uni. When he knocked on the door, her suitcase was still in the hall.

'You coming?' he asked, and under the orange porch light, he flashed her the stout bottle in his pocket.

Things had changed. She'd been away for three months. Seen things, done things. 'We're all just having a cup of tea,' she said. 'Why don't you come in and say hi?'

He glanced behind her and they listened for a moment to her parents doing the dishes in the kitchen. Before he spoke again a gust of wind came and she had to brace the door. A gale had got up that afternoon, blowing from the north. All the way from the train station it had swiped at her dad's owld Transit. She heard it now in the birch, the thrashing branches like the sound of the sea. Malcolm looked into the wind, screwed up his eyes.

'So you coming?'

The same words, the same voice.

'I've got stuff to unpack,' she said.

She wished she had gone. As soon as she closed the door and realised it was just her and her mam and dad, an evening of Corrie and Taggart, she wished she had gone.

It is after dinner that Moira appears.

'Sarah!' she says. 'And are you staying?'

Moira always asks this. Sarah smiles but avoids Moira's eyes. Her feelings for Moira are wrapped in the guilt of that last conversation with her son. 'Just the bank holiday,' she says.

'I've a lamb stuck, Elsie. Would you ever come and help?'

'Of course we will. Come on, Sarah,' her mam says, pulling on her wellies. The three of them walk up by the Munro place, setting the dogs barking, and then across the common grazing, every inch of it scattered with sheep muck. 'Where did you say it is?' Sarah's mam asks. But Sarah already knows where the lamb is. Far across the ragged ground, the sea whispers somewhere, unseen. When they get to the crag, the yowe is standing at the edge, bleating for its wee one. It's a Blackface, with tight little horns like seashells. There are others around the drying poles, grazing between the nets.

What is it Sarah really remembers after all this time? Their growing up together – it's all just fragments. Memories like ticket stubs found in an old wallet. Or else in their mundanity (days walking to school, nights sitting on the crag), the memories are stuck together like tissues, the layers refusing to be picked apart.

'Hello, little one,' Moira says, bending down at the spot where Sarah and Malcolm used to sit. It's a forty-foot drop to the boulders below. For years you'd been able to see where the edge had crumbled, the sward pulled away. The lamb is stuck on a jut, which means someone will have to lie down to reach it.

'Sarah,' her mam says.

The sheep around the drying poles stop eating. Slowly, they come to watch, heads bowing here and there. Sarah gets down on her chest. She sees the edge, her own hands in the short grass, the quivering eyebright. She sees the skinny white body of the lamb, the legs braced against the rock. It is nothing like that night. It is summer. There is hardly any wind. The sea is calm. Looking down, she feels cheated. It should have been more terrifying; instead, the lamb is just an arm's scoop beneath her and she knows its fleece will feel warm in her hands. Sure enough, with her fingers spread under its chest, she can feel its trembling, so irrelevant, and the tapping of its tiny heart.

'There,' she says, crawling backwards, and she sees now that Moira has also lain down and is ready to take the lamb from her. They look at each other a minute. Sarah's chest feels damp and her heart is beating hard.

The yew doesn't stop to give thanks. She totters off with the lamb twined around her hind legs. Is that it? Will Sarah go back now and watch telly with her mam? Eat chocolate digestives and go to bed with a hot water bottle. She was scared she would see him there on the rocks. Some idea of how his limbs had lain, a stain of sorts. But there was nothing.

Back at the house, Sarah tells her mam she's going to sit outside for a bit. When later that night the wind gets up, she realises she has run out of memories. Rewound them all so many times the tape has stuck. She has searched for him everywhere and the only time she found him was tonight, looking into his mam's eyes. All she herself has is a feeling – a shadow that moves when she turns towards it. Still, every time she comes back here, that's what she does. She keeps turning towards it, keeps trying to catch it out. Sitting on the garden bench, given up on thinking, her arms and legs feel heavy.

The barn door creaks. The breeze is cold on her face. With all the cloud, dusk falls early, and Sarah looks about, realising the yard is on the cusp of darkness. There is a clanking sound over by the fence. Clank, clank, clank. She doesn't need daylight to know what it is. There's an old water tank on its side in the grass and a boat trailer, its handles tie-wrapped with bits of rubber, the winch strap dangling and the hook clanking off the frame. Back and forth in the wind. And even though it's too dark to see, she knows the exact angle the trailer lies against that owld tank. They've sat there for years, the tank unused and the boat long sold, the grass around them long where the mower can't go.

When she turns there is a light on in the kitchen and her mam is standing at the window. Her face is too much in shadow to tell her expression but still Sarah feels something pass between them – her mother in there in the light and Sarah's eyes getting used to the dark.

Laura Morgan is previously published in The Moth, Causeway/Cabhsair, and Northwords Now, and has been long and short-listed for various competitions, including the Brighton Prize, the Colm Tóibín Short Story Award, and the Bristol Short Story Prize. In 2015, she was shortlisted for the Scottish Book Trust's New Writers Awards.

Blog: aremoteview.wordpress.com

About The Hysterectomy Association

The Hysterectomy Association provides impartial, timely and appropriate information and support to women. It was founded in the mid 1990's by Linda Parkinson-Hardman who is the author of several books about hysterectomy, online business and one novel.

It is based in Dorset in the UK and you can find out more about the association through the following accounts:

Website: hysterectomy-association.org.uk
Facebook: facebook.com/HysterectomyUK
Twitter: twitter.com/HysterectomyUK
LinkedIn: linkedin.com/company/the-hysterectomy-association

Hysteria UK can be found online at www.HysteriaUK.co.uk

Other books from The Hysterectomy Association include:

- 101 Handy Hints for a Happy Hysterectomy
- In My Own Words: Women's Experience of Hysterectomy
- Losing the Woman Within
- The Pocket Guide to Hysterectomy
- A Diva's Guide to the Menopause - Short Story
- Hysteria 1
- Hysteria 2
- Hysteria 3
- Hysteria 4

You can connect directly with Linda, our editor, on her blog at www.womanontheedgeofreality.com.

★ D I D 1 6 6 9 7 6 3 ★

#0173 - 291116 - C0 - 210/148/7 - PB - DID1669763